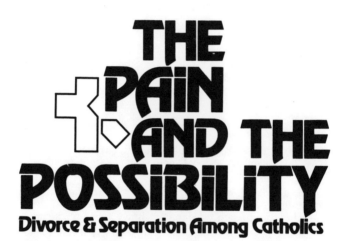

# THE PAIN AND THE POSSIBILITY

## Divorce & Separation Among Catholics

---

# PAULA RIPPLE, F.S.P.A.

AVE MARIA PRESS    NOTRE DAME, IND. 46556

**Special Note**

This book has been written in relation to real experiences shared with real people. The experiences have been altered and generalized in such a way as to protect and respect the privacy of persons as well as my own professional commitment to confidentiality.

In any instance where a person might be recognizable, individual permission has been obtained.

The selections in the chapter "How Do the Divorced View Marriage?" were written for specific use in this book.

First printing, September, 1978
Fourth printing, December, 1981
42,000 copies in print


Acknowledgments:

Excerpts from the Introduction by Thomas Merton to *To Live Is to Love,* by Ernesto Cardenal, copyright © 1974 by the Seabury Press, Inc. Reprinted by permission of The Merton Legacy Trust.

From "East Coker" in *Four Quarters* by T. S. Eliot, copyright © 1943 by T. S. Eliot; copyright © 1971 by Esme Valerie Eliot. Reprinted by permission of Harcourt Brace Jovanovich, Inc.

From *Letters to a Young Poet* by Rainer Maria Rilke, copyright © 1934 by W. W. Norton & Company, Inc., New York. Translation by M. D. Herter Norton. Reprinted by permission of W. W. Norton & Company, Inc.

All royalties from this book go to the North American Conference of Separated and Divorced Catholics.

Cover design by Cae Esworthy
Art by Jack Lindstrom, Minneapolis, Minnesota

Printed and bound in the United States of America.

# Contents

For my father and mother who,
by the way they lived much more
than by any words they spoke,
taught me what it means to love
and care for others.

# Foreword

Paula Ripple understands so well the special pain and heartache a divorced person experiences. Her sensitivity and compassion tell us something quite profound about being human—that all of us at the deepest layers of our humanity are one, and if we connect with one another there in the depths, we find bonds of understanding and communication we never could have imagined.

Paula is also a woman of imagination. Her capacity to put herself in the place of a man or woman who has been rejected, someone who is anxious about today and tomorrow, has made her an unusually effective divorce minister.

While she was a parish minister in suburban Minneapolis, Paula helped start a support group for divorced men and women. She later helped establish an archdiocesan center for divorced Catholics, and for the past

year has been Executive Director of the North American
Conference of Separated and Divorced Catholics, an organ-
ization led by divorced Catholics themselves. In her new
post Paula has worked tirelessly to promote the development of this much-needed ministry in the U.S. and Canada.

This book is just what the divorced Catholic needs.
In an easy-to-read style, Paula illuminates all the special
problems, puzzles, pains and strengths of being a divorced
Catholic. It is a thoughtful, prayerful book which will
bring the reader almost as much peace and healing as
meeting Paula herself.

**James J. Young, C.S.P.**
*Chaplain, North American Conference of*
*Separated and Divorced Catholics*

# 1. Is Divorce A Beginning or An End?

> *"Here, then, I have today set before you life and prosperity, death and doom. If you obey the commandments of the Lord, your God, which I enjoin on you today, loving him and walking in his ways and keeping his commandments, you will live and the Lord, your God, will bless you in the land you are entering to occupy . . . I call heaven and earth today to witness; I have set before you life and death, blessing and curse. Choose life, then, that you and your descendants may live."*
>
> *Deuteronomy 30:15-16,19*

When I think of our invitation to CHOOSE LIFE, I think of two divorced Catholics. They were the last two people that I saw one afternoon just before I left my office. The first was Ted who was 23. The second was Joe who was 73.

Ted had come to see me at the request of his mother. She had called and asked to talk to me about her son. She was sad and somewhat disturbed by the fact that her youngest son, her "baby," was now divorced. She said she found it very difficult to accept him in her home and that she was even uncomfortable at family meals since he moved home following his separation. She admitted her own need for help in understanding her son's broken marriage. She was also concerned about the way in which he was dealing with his failure. The last words Ted said to me as he left my office that day were, "What's left for me? I'm 23 and I'm divorced. It seems to me as if my life has ended."

As I walked to the door with Ted, Joe was just coming in. Joe was probably divorced at about the same age as Ted. He was remarried. He had raised all of his children as Catholics. He had sent them to Catholic schools and colleges. He had gone to Mass every Sunday. His Lutheran wife had not been able to join the Church. Like so many other divorced/remarried Catholics, Joe had sat in the pew every Sunday as the people all around him approached the altar for communion. Joe asked, "Is there any way that you can help me? I am not a young man anymore and I have not been feeling well lately. My dream is that I will be able to receive communion before I die."

Joe and I began to talk about his marriage, his life, his faith, his need for God and for prayer. We talked about marriage, what it is that blesses a marriage and what faithfulness in marriage means. We talked about God and faithfulness to God's ever-present invitation to new life. As we were finishing our conversation, I could see Joe growing more relaxed and feeling better about himself. He even said to me, "May I call my wife while I'm still here? May I tell her that we have finally found someone who understands, someone who has helped me feel good about my marriage after all these years?" When Joe left my office, he put his arms around me and said to me, "I feel like my whole life is just beginning."

What is the difference between these two good men? Why does Ted, at age 23, look upon divorce as an end and how can Joe, at age 73, view his life as just beginning?

The answer to that question rests in the realization that whether we view human experience, however painful, as a beginning or an end does not depend on forces, events or circumstances outside ourselves. It is not friends and neighbors and relatives, nor is it a pastor or someone else in the Church who can make this important decision for us. It is not even God who decides.

The answer to that question rests on our realization of our personal responsibility to determine the direction of our lives. It resides in a conviction of faith that God is present in the events of our lives as we write our human stories. God's presence is like a loving environment surrounding us always. It is a presence larger than we are, a presence that gives strength and hope for new life.

We are called continually to new life. We are called to make new beginnings. Sometimes we miss the meaning of human life because we fail to take time to reflect on the simple daily experiences that are ours. We need to think about our lives and what they mean. When we do, we realize that one of the most human and humanizing beliefs is that God continually invites us to CHOOSE LIFE.

The seasons of the year, the beauty of the earth, the process by which things grow, remind us that all of life is a series of endings and beginnings. We know that the endings and the beginnings are related processes and that one does not happen without the other.

We continually make new beginnings. Some of them

are very undramatic. Young children go to school for the first time. Students graduate from high school or college and leave home to go to work. People are married, or ordained, or enter religious communities and so make new beginnings. We change jobs, we move, and, if we think about it, we realize that there are few things that we are called to do more frequently. There are few things that hold more potential meaning for life than the new beginnings that we make.

How is it that we have been ensnared in a contradiction that would have us believe that sometimes we can make new beginnings, but that the new beginning process is selective? Where have we gotten the information that we can begin again with some decisions of life but not with others?

It is clear that this message could never have been given to us by God. God calls us to new and renewed life always as the words of Deuteronomy tell us: "I set before you life and death. Choose life . . ." It is a matter of great personal responsibility. This is what we are called to do.

New beginnings are an invitation to us to take charge of the meaning and direction of our lives. We might understand what this means with even greater clarity if we ask ourselves the question: how have I felt when someone made it very clear to me that I could not begin again?

I talked recently to a woman who had just come from a visit to her pastor. Her parish is like parishes all over the country. It is like the human church to which we belong. Her pastor's response to her divorce situation was that he saw no hope for her. He told her that her divorce was, as far as he was concerned, the final thing in her life in the church. He said that there was very little that he could do for her. She experienced rejection and a feeling that she could not begin again in his parish. In her pain and confusion, she asked me, "How can that be? How is it that the church can heal me from every other human failing? Why is divorce a worse sin than murder or robbery?"

How do we feel when we are told that we cannot begin again? Our feeling for our life tells us that there is something dehumanizing about being told, "You cannot begin again." Somehow there is something very unchristian about the message that we cannot begin again. And, somehow, there is something untrue about that message.

Faithfulness to our understanding of who God is in our lives will tell us that we can begin again even though parents and friends and relatives and people in the Church and people we meet daily may want us to believe that we cannot. We can be sure that this is not what God is telling us.

Having asked how we feel when we cannot begin again, it is important for us to look at another face of that question and to ask ourselves, "How do I feel in the presence of people who tell me that I can always begin again?"

Sometimes it is our own inability to accept forgiveness from others that makes it impossible for us to receive the message of their ongoing acceptance and care. We may not believe in ourselves enough to believe that we can be forgiven. We may not know how to find the words to tell another that we are sorry for having failed. We may even have believed the myth of "Love means never having to say you are sorry."

We stand in need of forgiveness always. We need that forgiveness most from those to whom we are closest, those we hurt and by whom we are hurt in the very process of trying to understand our lives. Each need for forgiveness and each expression of this need is a loving act of trust.

The German theologian, Paul Tillich, has said that "Faith is accepting God's acceptance." At the heart of human love as well as of faith is our ability to accept ourselves and to believe in the acceptance of others.

We rely on family and friends to interpret for us in meaningful ways the clear message of God's covenant with us, a covenant of unconditional acceptance and unfailing love. In the Book of Genesis we read of God's promise of faithfulness to us:

> See, I set my rainbow in the heavens as a reminder of the covenant between me and the earth. When I bring clouds over the earth, and the rainbow appears in the clouds, I will remember the covenant I have made between me and you and all living things.[1]

We need friends like that, friends with whom we can begin again. We need the presence of people in our lives who remind us of God's message, "I set before you life and death. Choose life that you may continue to live."

Where do we look for models of new beginnings? Where do we look for heroes as we try to understand our human experience? We need some people to whom we can look. We need to be able to say, "If that person could do it, then so can I."

To find some people who have been "heroes" for many Christians, let's look at those who have helped us understand what the experience of new beginnings meant for them.

We begin with the Old Testament with a man named Jeremiah. By most human standards Jeremiah was not a likeable person. In his time, he was known as the "prophet of doom." The city of Jerusalem was under siege. In the

---

[1] Genesis 9:13-15

midst of the destruction, Jeremiah was searching to understand the direction of his life, to find its meaning to understand where the days of his life were leading him. In the
midst of the turmoil in the city of Jerusalem, a relative of
his named Hanamel came to Jeremiah to try to convince
him to buy some property in Jerusalem.

Jeremiah, in thinking about the offer, received the
message that Hanamel's invitation to buy property was
telling him where his life direction was. Jeremiah agreed to
buy that piece of property. The response of the people
around him must have been, "You can't be serious about
this. You can't be serious about buying a piece of property
in a city that is being destroyed."

Jeremiah not only bought the property, he invested
his life savings in doing so. And he said to them, "Vineyards will grow in this land again."

As I think about that story, I think of separated and
divorced people. I think of people whose lives, like the city
of Jerusalem itself, have been under siege and have seemed
near to complete destruction. But I have found that,
somehow, in their lives there is a seed of the same belief
that was there for Jeremiah. It is the belief that new life
will follow this destruction. "Vineyards will grow in this
land again."

Human hearts that have been wounded, that have
been hurt, that have, apparently, not been cared about,
these human lives which seemed to have failed will blossom
again. Jeremiah's life reminds us that we are called to
beginnings without end.

A second Old Testament figure whose life has an important message for us is Jonah. We remember Jonah as
the man who spent three days in the belly of the whale. We
have come to understand that the belly of the whale is
symbolic of the personal darkness in which Jonah walked.

It is the same darkness we know when we face important decisions. It is the darkness that we know when we try to understand where the Father's invitation to new life is leading us. The message of Jonah's story doesn't have anything to do with the belly of the whale. It has to do with the kind of person that Jonah was.

Jonah is called the "reluctant prophet." If Jonah had listened carefully to his life, he would have realized that he was being called to bring the message of repentance and salvation to the people of Nineveh.

Jonah did not want to go to Nineveh. He did not like the people of Nineveh. He refused to go there. He boarded a ship heading in the opposite direction. And that is the beginning of Jonah's story as we know it.

Jonah finally does go to Nineveh. He brings to its people there the realization they must repent. When they do repent, God is pleased with them. It is Jonah who has brought the message. But Jonah is angry with God. He is reluctant to the end. He did not want the people of Nineveh to receive the message of God's love.

The story of Jonah's reluctance reminds me of feelings I've felt in my own life as I've walked the streets of an unfamiliar city, sometimes wondering whether I had the strength and the courage to do what I had made a commitment to do. I have experienced in myself the feeling that the ideals and reality in my own life pull me in two different directions, as they did in the life of Jonah.

Finally, there is another Old Testament figure who has often been important to me during decision-making times. Times of leaving the total security of a place where I am loved and accepted to go into a "foreign land" to begin again, to make friendships and to find a new community. At such times the Bible on the table in my living room is open to a passage that relates the story of Abraham. Our

Christian roots rest with Abraham. Because he listened carefully to his own life, Abraham received God's call to life, "Leave your father's house and your friends and set out for a land that I will show you."

Separated and divorced Catholics had that experience when they married. They left family, friends and their father's house and set out for a land that was filled with hope and expectation for them. Somehow the hopes and expectations that were theirs as they set out for that foreign land, that new place of marriage, ended not to be the place of fulfillment for which they had hoped, but instead a place of pain and struggle. It is a place not understood, not even by those who loved them.

Reflection on the life of Abraham, whose courage and openness to new life made it possible for him to listen to God's call, can help us realize that beginnings without end are possible for us as they were for him.

Like Abraham, we can set out for a new life and a new land that will always be shown to us when we take seriously our responsibility to CHOOSE LIFE. We need to believe that we can make new lives for ourselves. We need to believe that we can count on God's love and that we will find in a loving community the support and caring for our lives that will sustain us as we "leave family and friends and set out for a land that will be shown to us."

Who are some of the people in the New Testament that speak to us of their own call to make beginnings without end? Who will show us how to make our response to life and how to be faithful to our call to choose life again and again?

Certainly one person who comes to mind is the impulsive Peter. He always needed forgiveness from the Lord. Peter who spoke and acted before he thought, Peter who even denied his friendship with Jesus at the time his faithfulness was most needed by Jesus, this same Peter receives Jesus' unconditional friendship and believes again that he is acceptable to Jesus even in the face of failure and lack of fidelity. Sorrow and forgiveness are the main character- istics of Peter's story.

Peter shows us in a very human way that the face of the Father is revealed to us through the human companions and through our own human lives which tell us that we can do in our lives what others have done.

One of the most painful things for the separated and divorced is the conflict between the personal belief that they did everything they could to make the marriage a place of life and growth, and the judgment they often receive from others who look at their broken marriages, people who give them the feeling that they are failures because their marriages failed.

Their failure is not as clear and dramatic as Peter's. Often they do not really believe that they failed because they know what high personal investment they made. When these good people turn to their church for healing and help, it is often at that moment that they are made to feel guilty by the stereotypes that others carry about them.

In Jesus' relationship with Peter we find no limits. We hear no words from Jesus about certain failures being ac- ceptable and able to be forgiven while others are not. We hear only words of forgiving "even seventy times seven."

Jesus' ongoing friendship with Mary Magdalen por- trays for us again that friendship bonds are not destroyed because human ideals are not realized. In fact, it is as though Jesus is saying that for him the measure of his love and his faithfulness to his friends was related to the mag- nitude of the friend's failure. Mary Magdalen was a person struggling with her own humanness. She continually tried to put her life together in a way that had meaning for her.

Who of us can imagine what the presence of a person like Jesus meant to her as she struggled with a way to believe in herself and to understand her life?

Few separated and divorced people could claim the depth and extent of Mary Magdalen's failure. Yet we see Jesus manifesting a tenderness toward her that speaks of how much he values her life and her friendship.

These stories of Jesus' concern for his friends are sacred to us. They give us hope. They give us the courage to begin again. They give us the reassurance that there is no sin that cannot be forgiven and healed. These stories remind us to look upon ourselves as good people, loved by Jesus who shows us the way to his Father.

The story of the woman at Jacob's well is a story of the compassion of Jesus. The Jesus who asks this woman for a drink of water promises her the "living water" that only he can bring. The Jesus who speaks with this several times divorced woman sees the heart of the person and invites her to "begin again." He lets her know that she is lovable and that her life matters to him.

I do not personally know any separated and divorced person who has had such a long series of failed marriages. But I know many separated and divorced people whose sense of self-worth has been much more devastated than was the Samaritan woman's. What a difference the presence of a person like Jesus made to her, Jesus who affirmed her personal worth by promising her "living water."

It is this "living water" that the separated and divorced seek from the church. They need to know that they can come to the church for strength and healing and the reassurance that there is a difference between a failed marriage and being a failure as a human being.

As we think of these stories of Peter and Magdalen and the woman at Jacob's well, we find in Jesus himself the

final and lasting message of beginnings without end. Jesus
was, in a human way, the ultimate failure. Even his closest
friends spoke of him on the road to Emmaus as "the one
we had hoped would have saved Israel." Jesus walked
through his own death and resurrection and in doing this
he helps us walk through our own personal pain and failure
to new life and strength. Easter was a day of new beginning for Jesus.

What are we saying as we pursue the question of
beginnings without end? What are we saying as we en-
courage one another to look at the lives of those who show
us that we can always begin again? They show us that our
faithfulness to our Christian commitment not only allows
us to start over, but demands that we do so.

We find the goodness and beauty of the earth with its
changing moods and seasons reminding us of our challenge to choose life again and again. The changes in the
earth, like the events of our lives, are sometimes quiet and
nearly unnoticed, like the leaves falling quietly as fall
becomes winter. After the seeming inactivity of winter,
the earth bursts forth dramatically telling us that another
spring has come. The new life and growth proclaim that
winter's life was strong and faithful, as transition times in
our own lives remind us that we were stronger than we
knew, and that life emerges in us in ways not unlike those
of the earth.

The transition times in our lives, times of new risk,
times of personal uprooting, are doorways to new and
richer life for us. The courage to leave the known and walk
into the unknown, like the transitions in nature from sum-
mer to fall or winter to spring, becomes a certain route to
renewed or new life. But if we are afraid to let go of what
we know, even when it is destructive to us, we cannot claim
faithfulness to life, nor will we ever feel the excitement of

new life bursting forth in us.

We find the promise and the hope for these transition times in God's own promise of faithfulness to us. His promise to be with us as he was with the ancient Hebrews in their journeys as they continued to set out for a land that God would show them.

When we make choices for life that are painful and that take us to some "foreign land," some place of new discovery for us, we carry with us the ever-present question, "What if I make a decision that asks more of me than I can give? Do I have the personal strength I need to walk into the unknown?"

At such times we can remember God's own words to us, "I set before you life and death . . . CHOOSE LIFE. . . ." And, with this invitation is God's own promise of a presence to be with us. That presence strengthens our belief that life is at once a gift and a promise of the courage and hope that we need if we are to be faithful to our own lives, and faithful to God.

I do not suggest that new beginnings are simple or easy or comfortable. They are challenging and they are terrible, and I speak out of my own experience as you could speak from yours. I also know, when I reflect on my own life, that every time that I have believed that God's acceptance and love are present, and that even in the darkness in which I walked I was responding to God's invitation to life, then I know that, at those times, I have had the courage to choose life again. I do this knowing that, like separated and divorced people who know well the winter of their lives, the call to make beginnings without end is certain and renewing.

T. S. Eliot summarizes this message in a poem called "East Coker."

Home is where one starts from.  As we grow
    older
The world becomes stranger, the pattern more
    complicated
Of dead and living.  Not the intense moment
Isolated, with no before and after,
But a lifetime burning in every moment
And not the lifetime of one man only
But of old stones that cannot be deciphered . . .
Love is more nearly itself
When here and now cease to matter . . .
We must be still and still moving
Into another intensity
For a further union, a deeper communion
Through the dark cold and the empty desolation,
The wave cry, the wind cry, the vast waters . . .
In my end is my beginning.[1]

---

[1] "East Coker," *The Complete Poems and Plays,* T. S. Eliot (New York: Harcourt, Brace and World), p. 129.

# 2. Who Are The Divorced?

*This treasure we possess in earthen vessels to make
it clear that its strength comes from God and not
from us. We are afflicted in every way possible,
but we are not crushed; full of doubts, but we
never despair. We are persecuted but never
abandoned; we are struck down but never
destroyed.*

*II Corinthians 4:7-9*

Five years ago I met the first divorced Catholic that I
had ever known. I had given a talk called *Self-Acceptance:
The Key to Relationships.* At the end of the evening a
young man asked if he could make an appointment for the
following week. I remembered having seen him at Sunday
Mass. He was very attractive—the kind of appearance that
people notice. I had wondered how long he'd be coming to

Mass alone. . . . Like the rest of the world, my mind, more at that time than now, instinctively thought of the world in twos.

When John came to see me the following week, he told me his story. It was the painful story of a marriage that had begun the previous September and had ended with a divorce the following May. As I sat across from John feeling so keenly the pain in him, aware of his near inability to speak about the failure of a relationship that had touched him as a person, as a man, as a friend, it was clear that no facet of his life had escaped the shattering. How aware I was that his treasure was carried "in an earthen vessel."

As he continued to share his experience with me, I was conscious of another process that was going on inside me. It was as though one after another of my stereotypes of divorced people was passing in review.

John said, "I gave my whole life, all of me, to this relationship. I loved Cathy, and all of my energy was invested in having a marriage that would last as long as we lived." I thought of how often I had heard the words that "divorced people don't believe in marriage anyhow"; that the divorced are people who just "try it out" but never intend that it last; that divorced people don't take seriously the words of Jesus about the permanence of marriage. These words and many others like them just didn't fit anymore as I realized that the reason why John was so devastated was that something he had chosen for his life had not been possible as he had believed and dreamed. Had he valued marriage less, it would have been much easier.

I needed more time to think about all the implications of his words, but he was saying to me, "I was born and raised a Catholic in a good Catholic family. I went to Mass and communion and did all the other things that good Catholics do. I am not sure how much any of that really meant to me. Prayer had never seemed that important. But, when my marriage fell apart, when I realized that there was nothing that I could do to change that, when I experienced my own inability to do anything about my relationship with Cathy, I felt a need for God that I had never known before. I began to pray. I discovered that my faith was much more important to me than I had ever realized." And, as he talked, I was remembering the words that I had often heard attached to the divorced—words like "unfaithful," "people without religion," "people who don't pray," "people who don't believe in God." How often have we heard it said, "If you had been a better Catholic you could have made your marriage work." "Good Catholics don't get divorced."

But this person's life was telling me something different from that. John explained to me that, at first, he had felt guilty about turning to God because, even though he had done all the things that good Catholics do, he had never before experienced his own need for God in so dramatic a way. And now, he was turning to the church for healing and support for his life. He was reaching out to someone in the church to help him put his life back together again.

Each time John came into my office he would ask, "Well, before we begin, what does that Loving Father you always talk about have to say to us today?" We would read some short passage from God's Word. Then John would say to me, "This is what he's been telling me this past week," and he would play for me some contemporary song and tell me what the words meant to him and to his life. He would tell me what they said to him about God. How many people would be surprised at the profound sense of prayer in a young divorced man, when the images they carry of the divorced do not portray them as a prayerful people, close to God and searching for the meaning of their own lives?

As we talked, John asked for four more meetings with me. He said that he was afraid that if we didn't set the dates he might not come back. He said, "I'm sure I'm going to hear some things from you that I may not want to hear. I'm sure we'll ask some questions that will be difficult to answer. I'll learn some things about myself that I may not like." The notion that divorced Catholics come to the church looking for easy answers passed through my mind. But here was a person committed to asking the difficult questions, open to the pain of questioning, not wanting to find some false security in failing to take his own life seriously.

It was disconcerting to hear a man of 22 saying, "How can I ever love someone again? How do I know that the same thing won't happen?" The image of the divorced as people who easily and quickly move in and out of marriage came to mind. To hear a person, who had chosen marriage as a way of life, questioning his future, doubting his ability to share lifelong companionship with some special person in his life, was another reminder of how superficial and how inaccurate the impressions are that people often have of the divorced. People seem to form their impressions of who gets divorced from what they read in the newspaper or what they see on television, and not from the lives of faithful, searching people. The images conveyed through the media often have little to do with the separated and divorced who are seeking healing and support from the church.

Through those next weeks John asked some questions about the annulment process. He said, "The church is becoming more and more important to me. If I ever do want to get married again, I hope it can be in the church."

I remembered talking with a woman just the week before who had said, "If divorced people really cared about the church, they wouldn't be divorced in the first place. I can't imagine that an annulment means much to them." How easily people decide about other people's lives.

Part of the assumption that an annulment wouldn't make much difference to most divorced people is the notion others have that all divorced people are angry and bitter about life in general, but, especially they are angry and bitter with the church. While it is true that the church has often not been the place of healing and compassion that the separated and divorced had hoped, and while it is also true that often the most severe judgments are levelled against the divorced by righteous Christians, it is clear that the separated and divorced who come to the church seeking healing and a home love the church with a fidelity that is all too uncommon in the total Christian community.

Now, five years later, as I look back on those hours John and I spent together, I see him as the beginning of a long series of good people, divorced people, who, because they shared their painful stories with me, removed my own stereotypes. They have helped me to change the attitudes of others by my sharing of the experiences that have been shared with me.

When I ask the question now, "Who are the divorced?" I think of names and individual lives, not categories and generalizations. I see the divorced as people "afflicted in every possible way, but not crushed."

The divorced are people like Roger, a young and gifted minister. He and Ruth had struggled with their marriage and been seeing counselors for nearly three years. In his last letter he said, "We just no longer had the energies to work on our relationship. The distance time provides now allows me to see the divorce as more therapeutically growthful than I could ever have accepted a year or two ago."

The divorced are people like Leo—a man from a large family. He told me that when he and his brothers and sisters were growing up they lived down the street from a divorced woman. His mother told them to stay away from her house and never to accept candy or cookies from her because "She's a bad person. She is divorced and I don't want you near her." When Leo's own marriage didn't work out after more than 10 years, when his divorce was final, he found himself thinking about himself in those same ways. He also realized that his whole family thought about him like the description of "the divorced woman down the street." Now, a few years later, Leo's first marriage has been annulled, and he is remarried but some members of his family continue to live with the attitudes towards divorced people that they developed as children.

The divorced are people like Rita whose husband left her when their last daughter left for college. Like so many others, Rita had been raised believing that the most important thing good married people can do is to be good parents. Neither her parents nor her church had helped her understand that married people are primarily friends and companions to each other. They are primarily people called to witness to the world the love of Christ for his church by the quality of their love for each other. Like so many people married 20 years or more, Rita and Larry had been so busy trying to be good parents that they were shocked to realize that, with their family gone, they were two strangers, living in the same house. They had not taken time, had not learned how to invest in the growth of their own friendship. The Marriage Encounter people like to use a banner at their weekends that says, "The most important thing a man can do for his children is to love their mother." Larry was not willing to begin to develop a friendship with the "stranger" he had lived with for so long.

The divorced are people like Steve whose wife had gone back to school to work for her master's degree. The longer she stayed in school the more involved she became in the feminist movement and the less she wanted any responsibility for their three sons. One day she came home and announced that she "wanted out" of any responsibility for home or children as of that very day. After the master's degree she began work on a doctorate, and so it continued. The divorce is final now and he has the children. Whatever else might be said, there is little evidence that either of them is a "bad person" or a person who started from some careless and faithless stance. Steve told me, "People grow and change. The cultural pressures on our marriage were heavy. We were raised with such clear-cut views of the place of the husband and the wife in a marriage."

The divorced are like a woman I met at a conference for the separated and divorced. The woman was in her early sixties. She told me that her husband had left their home just two days earlier. She had little hope that he would return. She said to me, "I don't want to be here. I hate being one of them. I hate the thought of being divorced. I've had so many negative feelings about divorced people all my life."

The divorced are like a woman I met at our national conference at Notre Dame. For 15 years she had lived with a man who now claims to be homosexual. She said she had feared this since a few days after their marriage. They had four sons. She said, "We didn't know some of the things then that we know now about homosexuality and I lived in fear of my own husband molesting my sons." She said it never occurred to her to seek an annulment. Even if she had, she feared that her husband would not have cooperated with the process. . . . She finally did get a divorce and did remarry without an annulment. For years she and her second husband, also a Catholic, had gone to Mass every Sunday but had not received the sacraments. She had just recently sought help with an annulment and looks forward now to receiving the Eucharist after so many years of "Mass without communion."

The divorced are sons and daughters of good families, families in which not only parents and brothers and sisters, but aunts and uncles and grandparents find it difficult to accept and understand, difficult to continue loving. I think of a woman who called me several years ago. She told me that she had lived all her life with certain attitudes towards divorced people. She had believed most of the things that people believe who have never known of the pain and self-destruction related to divorce. Now her 26-year-old daughter was in the process of separation. She said, "It's changing all the things I once thought about the divorced. I know my daughter is a good girl. I know she worked hard to make a go of that marriage. I know that she was faithful. I also know that for her to continue to try and make that marriage work by herself was destroying her. I admire her for doing the difficult thing. Certainly God cannot be displeased with her."

The divorced are good parents—people like 24-year-old Kevin who has the custody of his two and three-year-old daughters. He works 70 hours a week so that he can keep his children in one day-care center so that they won't be shifted from one baby-sitter to another. He finds ways to spend time with them so that they will grow up feeling secure because they know that they are loved.

What a world of attitudes is revealed in words that children hear or more often overhear from their teachers. "His parents are divorced." The implication is not that single-parenting presents a great challenge to a woman (or a man) trying to raise the children alone. The implication is that the child misbehaves because his mother is not a good woman and the fact that she is divorced proves this.

Every story is different. Every story is a reminder that we are human beings who live in our own human darkness and walk in the ways of the human Jesus. Every story of the thousands of divorced Catholics I have met is a reminder that no one of them fits any mold into which we have cast them. Every story speaks of the pain of the human journey—a journey that can bring each person new life and a deeper sense of the presence of God.

The divorced are people living in an age when the cultural pressures on marriage are greater than ever before. Someone has said that the pressures of our time have made the American family the "number-one disaster area."

Knowing something of these cultural pressures on marriage and family may provide some insight into the lives of the divorced while, at the same time, giving important information for the not-yet-married and the already-married.

The mobility of our society has had an impact on our former concept of the nuclear family. Statistics tell us that the average American family moves every four years, that one in four families moves every year and that 50% of all American families live more than a thousand miles from "home." While people who have considerable difficulty living in harmony with in-laws may consider this as positive information, the truth is that much of the former support from family and friends of a long time is now lacking. People search for support communities.

The feminist movement has had an impact on both home and marriage. It has drastically altered the nature of relationships between men and women. It challenges us to a time of "human liberation" when both men and women will live free of the culturally oppressive patterning which has distanced us from one another.

The phenomenon of working women began during World War II. When Rosie the Riveter went off to work to meet a need during a time of national crisis, the now-common practice of women working was begun. Women are becoming financially independent in a way they once were not. A woman who may have felt trapped in an unsatisfactory marriage because of economic reasons now no longer feels that pressure. The incidence of women leaving a home, a husband, a family is increasing. It is no longer uncommon to speak of "wife desertion."

People live longer now than they used to. As late as 1900 half of all American marriages ended in the premature death of one person, usually the woman, and usually in childbirth. That meant that a man sought a mother for his children and a wife for himself, often in that order. But, their span of time together was considerably shorter. Now, with longer life expectancy, even with the increased age for marriage, people can look forward to 50 years of married life. In a society where industries work hard at making things that will not last, in a society where much of what we use is throwaway, where disposability and easy replaceability are valued, it is difficult for the young to understand permanence and long-term commitments. It is difficult to put meaning around a church word like "indissolubility."

Certain "arrangements" such as triangle marriages, group marriages, open marriages, people living together before marriage—each of these is having an effect on marriage as we have known it. Each is a source of questions being asked by the married and the unmarried about the meaning of faithfulness and personal commitment.

A zero population growth mentality is affecting our understanding of marriage. Young people today are not only deciding when and how many children they will have, but whether or not they will have children at all.

The difficulty in purchasing homes because of economic pressures has never been so great. The home has been an important symbol of the stability of marriage and family. It has also provided the married with the psychological space needed to sustain and enrich a healthy friendship in marriage.

Our culture places heavy pressures on the young to marry. Even the very young are caught up into a couple-orientated mentality. We continue to use categories like bachelor and spinster to speak of those who do not choose to be marriage-oriented. Someone has said that too many people get married. We are known to be the most "marrying" nation in the world. Though this is gradually changing, we still live in a time when marriage is a nearly ever-present expectation. I think of a young divorced woman whose husband told her, "I should never have married you in the first place. I am a loner. I don't want to be married. I only got married in the first place because my parents made me feel like there was something wrong with me when I wasn't married at 25."

The increase in divorce rates and the ease in obtaining a divorce have caused more divorces. When it was more difficult to get a divorce, some people chose to invest some added energy in the marriage to try and "make it work." It is equally true that this former difficulty in obtaining a divorce sometimes kept people in marriages that were clearly destructive.

Too often we do not take a good look at the cultural pressures affecting marriage because we almost immediately set about moralizing about the cultural changes, mak-

ing judgments about the goodness or badness of the pressures. When we too quickly make "morality" the question,
we make a growthful assessment of situations nearly impossible. Much more helpful is the realization that these
and many other factors are putting tremendous pressures
on marriage as we have known it—marriage as Jesus
presented his ideal to us.

In addition to identifying the pressures, there is an
added and much more difficult invitation to us and to the
church. That is the need to look for creative ways to add
more realism and depth to both the practical and the faith
questions involved in marriage preparation. It challenges
the church to be more supportive of marriage itself by
taking seriously its responsibility for ongoing enrichment
for the already married. It is not enough to insist that
people participate in marriage preparation. The church
must provide the possibility of a support community, a
community sharing the common ideals given to us by Jesus
—ideals such as faithfulness, love, healing and the need
for continual growth.

Our consideration of the pressures affecting home and
family and marriage reminds me of a homily I once heard
on Holy Family Sunday. The priest giving the homily
suggested that the challenge to us on that Sunday was to
widen our understanding of the church, an understanding
often too narrow to be helpful. He invited us to widen our
understanding of church from that of the Holy Family
idea which has connotations of a small, intimate, unchanging circle. He suggested that the church is now invited
to look upon itself as WHOLLY FAMILY to those who
seek community in the church in ways that they cannot
any longer find "family" in society, among their associates
or even in their own neighborhoods.

As we have thought about the stereotypes that are all

too typical not only in our churches but in society in general, as we have asked ourselves who the divorced are, as we have looked at the cultural pressures that have affected the number of divorced, there is one single factor that touches on all of these and is so important that it deserves to be considered in and for itself.

Perhaps the single most important thing that we are learning from the separated and divorced as they share their experiences and their lives is that at the heart of the lives of the divorced and affecting these cultural pressures in its own unique way is the truth that expectations of marriage have never been higher than they are in our own time. In our age which has focussed on humanism and personalism, we have learned some important things about the growth of men and women in relationship. We have learned, in fact, that men and women do not grow except in relationships that are meaningful and challenging, as well as caring and faithful. We have learned that our faithfulness to God is woven into and is directly related to our ability to be faithful to one another. St. John tells us that, "No one has ever seen God" and the only measure we have of our love for God is the quality of our caring for one another.

Because we have come to know that our love for God and for each other is not separate, we realize that we don't do one well unless we are also doing the other. We find people no longer willing to stay in marriages where friendship either never was or has now become impossible. Having struggled with the difficult questions, often having sought the help of counsellors and others, the decision to leave a marriage is a response to the difficult realization that a friendship either never existed or may now be broken beyond healing. It is a response to the realization that to choose to stay in the marriage is to eventually be incapable of loving and accepting self, others and God.

The divorced people that I meet are faithful people who have come to understand that the treasure they possess in earthen vessels receives its strength from God. They have had the experience of affliction, doubt, persecution, abandonment, but they have not been destroyed. Out of the ruins of a broken marriage has emerged new and un-expected life.

# 3. How Do The Divorced Deal with Pain?

*My dwelling, like a shepherd's tent, is struck down and borne away from me. You have folded up my life, like a weaver who severs the last thread. Day and night yau give me over to torment, I cry out until dawn . . . like a swallow I utter shrill cries; I moan like a dove. My eyes grow weak, gazing heavenward; O Lord, I am in sadness; be my strength . . .*

*Isaiah 38:12-14*

Many scenes in the film *Equus* touched me deeply, but there is one that stands out above all others. It is the scene of a painful conversation between the mother and Martyn, the psychiatrist who is treating her son. With an anger akin to rage, she says to him, "You want to blame my husband and me for all that has happened to our son.

You want to say that we are responsible. Well, I want to tell you something. If you put together all the ways we have failed, all the things we didn't know how to do, all the ways we tried to love him and each other, but failed . . . If you put together all of that, it will not equal the evil of this terrible thing that he has done."

Somehow, divorce is like that. If you put together all the painful struggle that has been a part of two people trying to love each other, but, in the end, of failing, all of that pain and struggle cannot equal the terrible process, the trauma, the agony and the grief that follow when people begin to separate out two lives that they had once chosen to join. How well the words of Isaiah describe their pain, "My dwelling, like a shepherd's tent, is struck down."

I think of a call I received from a woman named Bernie. She needed reassurance as she said to me, "I think I'm losing my mind." She recounted to me the events of that afternoon. She had been separated only a few months and had been seeing a counsellor. That afternoon she told him that she was beginning to work out her hostility against her husband through her children. She said, "I find myself nagging at them and saying ugly things to them about their father in the hope that they will convey my messages to him." After spending time with her counsellor, trying to find constructive ways to deal with her feelings for her husband, she came home and began to clean the cupboards in the kitchen . . . The next thing she remembered, she was looking at an empty cupboard and a full set of broken dishes on the floor across the room.

What Bernie was struggling with was an intense phase of her own deep sense of personal loss. What she did not know, and what few separated and divorced people understand, is that they do, in fact, go through a grief process that somehow parallels the grief process that we experience when someone we love dies.

We are not concerned here with an academic debate about which hurts more, death or divorce. What is important is that all of us come to understand the grief process as it relates to our own lives, and to the lives of the people we care about.

Dr. Elisabeth Kubler Ross through her book *On Death and Dying* has deepened our understanding of grief. Her discussion of the grief process has helped us realize that we grieve for many things other than death. Following her work there have been articles written about the grief process as it relates to a woman having a mastectomy or a tubal ligation. Job loss, tooth extraction, moving, loss of youth, the burning of a home—all are related to the working out of some process of grief.

In our consideration of grief as it relates to the separated and divorced, it is important to focus on and emphasize the trauma of the process and not the particular steps or phases that one might experience. The disservice that can be done to the important contribution of Dr. Ross would be to have people begin to arrange their lives around what was intended to be a helpful exploration of grief when it touches human lives in a profound way.

When the works of writers grow popular, people misuse the helpful insights by making them final answers. It is frightening to meet people who are now writing their life script after reading Gail Sheehy's *Passages;* subconsciously almost programming their lives by what might have been a helpful understanding of the wider concepts of human growth and change.

One grief scholar has said that it is as basic as realizing that "When we lose something that is important to us, we grieve." Another has described grief as "the sociological, psychological, and physiological reaction to loss." Put

more simply, it is "the loss of someone or something that
we love or value."

When BLIZZARD '78 was reported in a Boston newspaper, one writer described the tragedy following the storm
and the cleanup. She said that the period of greatest difficulty begins now, in the time following the storm. She
predicted that many people would eventually need professional help in dealing with the losses they experienced. She
outlined three phases: Phase 1) during the storm people
were stunned and shocked; Phase 2) they got involved in
the task of survival, their own and that of others around
them; and Phase 3) the depression following the excitement
and strenuous physical activity. She was asking the important question, "Who helps now?"

As I read that writer's description of the physical
disaster that the storm was and the way in which it affected
the lives of thousands, one recurring thought was in my
mind. That thought was, "But divorce is so much more
terrible and terrifying. In death and in homes lost in
storms, there is not the feeling of personal rejection. There
is not the feeling of personal failure. There is not the guilt
and the feeling of having failed God as well as myself and
others."

It is never easy to let things and people that are important to us go out of our lives. This says something
about our ability to be faithful to what we have chosen.
We cherish ideas, things in which we have invested ourselves, but, most of all we cherish the people in our lives.
And, the more of ourselves that we have invested, the more
do we cling to that relationship which threatens to be lost.

T. S. Eliot in one of his poems says that we are a part
of all that we have met. We carry with us all the circumstances and events in our lives. In a singular way do we
carry with us all the relationships that have been important

to us. Nothing changes that. It does us no good to deny
a friendship that was once ours just because it did not
work out as we had once envisioned or hoped. That is why
is is important for us to understand something about the
grief process and how it affects us. This gradual process
provides the healthy coping mechanisms that we need to
deal with a severe and painful loss at a particular time in
our lives.

Because divorced people, like most other people, do
not understand the grief process, their pain is often greater
and their process of healing is longer and more destructive
than it might otherwise be. Once again the words of the
Prophet Isaiah seem meaningful and descriptive. "You
have folded up my life . . . like a swallow I utter shrill
cries. . . ."

I am reminded of a young divorced woman, the
mother of four children. She told me, "My children have
never cried, either before, during or after the divorce. But,
they are so nasty to each other. They fight all the time.
Sometimes it almost seems like they hate each other." As
we talked, I said, "Stephanie, have your children ever seen
you cry?" Then she explained, "I can't cry. I'm the
mother. I need to be strong for them." What she had done,
without realizing it, was to teach her children that you
walk away from a marriage of 14 years with no tears and
with no pain. She had denied them the healing they needed
for their own hurt and their opportunity to heal one
another.

Most of us have been programmed to deal with feelings in certain ways. Few of us have had an opportunity to
understand the experience of the grief process in ourselves.
We risk the possibility of being disappointed with ourselves
for responding in healthy and normal ways to pain and
loss. We do not understand that coping mechanisms are

both helpful and healing.

A woman named Jan told me, "This is the first time in my life that I have experienced what powerlessness means. Always before I could do something, always before I could make things work. Anything that I have ever wanted has been attainable for me. . . . But, I can't make this marriage work. My husband is gone and there is nothing that I can do except try to get my own life together again." Initially her rejection of her feelings of powerlessness brought her to a deep depression. It was her first experience of being, as she called it, "down," for a long period of time. This good woman had given herself generously to more than 20 years of marriage. Is it any wonder that she was feeling nearly destroyed now with the feelings of failure, powerlessness and depression so foreign to her?

The grief process that is experienced in divorce is not a single process. It is not clearly over at some particular point in time.

The divorce process is a multiple grief process. It involves mourning for the loss of not one relationship but many. In a divorce there is severance from the partner as husband or wife, as friend, as companion, as sexual partner, as provider, as person who kept the home, as one who shared responsibility for the children. This multiple loss process cannot be dealt with easily.

Psychologists speak of stress points and tell us that to be in a situation where more than two major things are changing at any given time in our lives is to be in a potentially precarious position for our own good mental health. We need time and understanding and the kind of gentleness with ourselves that can only come out of the belief that we are "normal" and somehow healing as the rest of the human race does.

There are dimensions of the grief process that continue for a very long time. I think of a widow who, several years after the death of her husband, called her son, crying and very much disturbed. When he asked her what was wrong she said, "When I woke up this morning, I realized that I could no longer remember the sound of your father's voice." And so the grieving continues. One who does not know this may add to someone's pain, or we may add to our own pain, by some of the overworked cliches that we use when we do not understand and therefore cannot be agents of our own healing. We use or hear words like, "I have to get myself together. I ought not be crying."

My father used to tell me that "our tears are like drops of holy water that bless and make holy our hurts and our struggles." Tears are an important part of a healthy human healing process. But we've been told so often that "big people don't cry," especially if the big people are men.

Paul Bohannan in an article called *The Six Stations of Divorce* speaks of the six different aspects of the divorce experience, any one of which has the potential of causing a major disruption in our lives. He speaks of an emotional divorce which centers around the problem of a deteriorating marriage. This involves the partners withholding their emotions from the marriage because the personal cost is too high. The emotional divorce may be complete long before the initial separation. There is the legal divorce. For many this is the first experience of the complicated court and legal process. The legal divorce is a frightening and difficult process for those for whom this is a first time in the courts. There is the economic divorce. Married people usually share money and property. In the divorce process the economic separation is often one of the most difficult and it is sometimes the area in which many feelings related to the other person are acted out. Fear of the economic divorce has kept many people from seeking an end to a broken marriage. Divorce often deals with custody and child visitation. It deals with going from a two-parent to a single-parent home. Responsibilities can no longer be shared as they once might have been. Community divorce is related to the changes which follow in former friend communities, places where two people once fit into social relationships. All too often divorce means the loss of an important set of relationships with friends. Psychic divorce challenges one to a process of growing alone and in a new way. It removes the ability to depend on someone else. Some people never make this psychic break. Years later lives are not separated out. The reality is yet denied.

Is it any wonder that divorced people often say, as did Dana, "I feel as though my arms and legs are being severed from my body, one by one. I feel like I am falling apart, and there's not a whole lot to hold me together these days." Not one relationship but many are terminated in every divorce.

No person ever "gets over" a death or a divorce or a limb amputation or any other major loss suffered. To expect that we will or should is to jeopardize our own healing process. A marriage, even if failed and ended, remains a part of two people's journey.

The normal grief process for death or divorce takes up to two years, but it may take longer. There is no way to hurry the process, no way to bypass the pain by simply "trying harder." Time is an important factor in the healing process, but time alone does not heal. Time only heals when people seek help and healing beyond themselves, in a community of friends and in faithful response to life. Time only heals when we value our own lives and believe in our ability to find new life.

The more the person we lost once meant to us, the greater the grief and the more difficult the healing process. The more of self that has been invested in any relationship, the greater the personal cost whether the loss is through death, divorce, or failed friendship. The dearer the ideal of lasting marriage, the more sincere the desire for companionship in marriage, the greater the pain of loss.

Extreme emotional responses are normal and healthy but they are also frightening for people who be experiencing such fitful emotional states for the first time in their lives. The grief process involves important human coping mechanisms. Bernie and her set of broken dishes and her subsequent terror at what she had done speaks primarily to our own common lack of understanding about human feelings and how we deal with them. People who have never before experienced human failure are often paralyzed with fear because of the intensity of their feelings.

The journey through the grief process enriches some lives and impoverishes others. People come to know that if they don't love very much, if they do not make themselves vulnerable, they will not hurt as much. The same grief process that opens some to life may be for others the beginning of a life that resolves to avoid human closeness in the future.

An intense grief process can add a depth and richness that gives life its own singular kind of beauty. We sometimes sense, in meeting others, that a particular person has some special quality that speaks about depth and openness and sensitivity. When we meet such a person we instinctively know that suffering has been a part of that life. Suffering can teach and temper as can no other human experience. It can make caring and gentle people of those who choose to respond. I once heard a psychologist named John Brantner describe the human journey as the making of a beautiful tapestry. Those whose lives are lived in the primary colors have a goodness and beauty that we value. But those who have suffered and who have not been broken or embittered by their pain are those whose tapestry has the richer darker hues, hues that speak of fullness of life. It is the gentle symbol of Isaiah when he says, "I moan like a dove . . . my eyes grow weak . . . I am sad."

It is important for us to understand the grief process and to reflect on it. If we don't know about the process of human response to loss, if we blame and reject ourselves or others because we haven't widened our own understanding of the coping mechanisms that are normal to and healthy in dealing with grief, then we will not be able to care about ourselves or others. We will not be able to walk through our own grief without being fractured unnecessarily.

A hospital handbook describes the *Coping Mechanisms in the Stages of Dying* as follows:

> *Shock*—Upon learning of his terminal diagnosis, the patient will usually become dazed and enter a state of disbelief. The initial comment of "Not me, it cannot be true," usually lasts only a short period of time.
>
> *Denial*—Death is hard to face. Patients say, "No, not me." The denial stage functions as a buffer. It allows the patient to collect himself and prepare other less radical defenses.
>
> *Anger*—Patients ask "why me?" "why now?" Their anger is usually directed at fate or God rather than at an individual. They focus their anger on forces for causing their untimely and unjust situation.

*Bargaining*—This is a helpful, if brief stage. The patient now says, "Yes, it is me—but . . ." which may postpone the inevitable. It may be the mother who just wants to be alive until her daughter's wedding or her son's graduation.

*Depression*—When the patient can no longer deny his illness, as his symptoms increase, he begins to experience a sense of great loss. The patient faces the truth of "Yes, it is me." It can be physical loss, as with amputation; financial loss, as due to mounting hospitalization costs; and/or personal loss, as he faces the impending absence of love objects.

*Acceptance*—If a patient has been given enough time and help in working through the other stages, he will reach a plateau at which he is neither depressed nor angry about his fate. At this time, he will be ready to die with peace and dignity. It should not be mistaken for a happy stage. It can be almost devoid of feeling. The patient is weaker and has a more pronounced need for sleep.

Let's take the description of these coping mechanisms as applied in dealing with death and translate them in terms of the divorce process. We do this with a reminder that it is not the naming and delineating of the stages that are important but rather the possible helpfulness of some systematic consideration which may evoke understanding or deeper insight for us.

**Shock**

When people announce that they are leaving (or, as sometimes happens, when one person leaves) the marriage, a response I have heard described by many divorced people was their own initial lack of feeling, their own numbness, their own inability to respond in any way.

Ted told me that he was out in the garage working on his car. His wife came out to announce to him that she was leaving, that she was in the house packing her bags. He said, "I can't believe it how I reacted. I just kept working on the car. By the time I came into the house, a couple of hours later, she was gone. . . . She was also furious, I found out later, because she thought I didn't care because I didn't stop working on the car. . . ."

Usually some reality factor, like a person leaving or the need to tend to other practical necessities, brings one out of the initial shock. When one person has left, the sudden change in the life of the other breaks through the initial numbness.

Sometimes, one person has been grieving long before the separation or divorce ever happens. When this is so, the process of healing may seem shorter because one or both of the partners have been dealing with the pain all along. One person may be aware of "losing" the other long before any discussion of separation.

## Denial

"Not our marriage. Not us." The denial has often gone on long before the separation. People refuse to notice that their marriage is in trouble. It becomes easier to ignore even well-set patterns or noncommunication. Walls are so easy to build and so difficult to remove. Vulnerability is never an easy demand.

Roberta told me that the day she received a call from the public health office asking her to come in for a VD check she told the caller that he had the wrong number and hung up. It was only when he called back to check on her name and phone number that she remembered that every day for the past several weeks, when she opened the cabinet in the bathroom, she had looked at a bottle of an antibiotic that she knew her husband was taking. She was a nurse and knew what the antibiotic was for. She denied it even to herself.

Marie struggled with her own disbelief at the extent of her denial mechanism. She had picked up her husband's wallet one day and had found there a contraceptive. She then promptly put the incident out of her mind—knowing full well that they never used them. . . . What frightened her most was the extent of her total surprise when her husband finally told her that he was leaving and that there was someone else in his life. So completely had she blocked what she did not want to know. . . . So complete was her denial.

Bill told me that he had gone to a travel agent to make reservations for a trip to the Carribbean for him and his wife to celebrate their 25th wedding anniversary even though she had already moved out and had the papers served for the divorce.

One couple I know has been separated for more than six months. They still go home to his parents and to hers for holidays and other family celebrations. They have told no one that they are separated.

It is significant that this denial process allows the person some of the time needed to get in touch with personal strengths. It carries with it, as do the other phases, the potential either for healing and growing through, or for destruction because of being locked forever into the shock or denial. This is true of any of the other stages. A person may choose, even subconsciously, not to deal with reality. A person can choose not to deal with life.

## Anger

"I'm really mad at God. Why did he let our marriage fall apart? When I lose something that is important to me and when I don't know how to deal with the loss, anger and blaming are common defenses. If I can blame God or my mother-in-law or the other person then I will never have to ask myself the painful questions about me."

"I stayed in this marriage for all those years and this is how God blesses me for having lived with an alcoholic who has harmed both me and my children." Marie remembers now having said this to me. That was before she came to realize that two people contribute to the patterns that exist in a marriage. Two people choose to stay in a marriage. What Marie had not done earlier was to question how it could be a loving thing for her to allow him to destroy his life by enabling his illness. The thing she had not done was to confront him with her own refusal to be an ongoing part of his self-destruction.

Anger and blaming God, or a mother-in-law, or the other person are sometimes an important part of the healing process. A key to this phase is how we deal or fail to deal with anger and whether anger is an acceptable or unacceptable feeling for us. Bernie's set of broken dishes threatened to destroy her until she learned that even expressing anger is sometimes healing.

The more something has meant to us, the greater is our frustration level when we risk losing it. Fitful emotional states, and the fear we often have at the intensity of our anger, are reminders to us of the way we have been programmed by our culture to view anger as an unacceptable feeling. This is especially true for women who have learned well that "nice women" never get angry, and certainly never express that anger. People are often most angry with themselves for having stayed too long in a marriage that was destructive for both of them. They are angry about their contribution to what they see, too late, as having been destructive of something they valued.

### Bargaining

"I'll be a different person if you'll just stay. I'll change." Sometimes the bargaining is with God. "I'll pray more. I'll begin to go to Mass every day."

Whatever form the bargaining takes, it is a shortsighted but sometimes necessary part of gradually dealing with loss. It doesn't take a long time for at least one person to realize that what is being bargained for is not what is at the heart of the problem in the marriage. For an alcoholic to stop drinking, for someone who has had the pattern of not coming home several nights a week to begin coming home every night, is not touching the question that is central to the problem.

One reason that this bargaining is difficult to deal with may be because the pattern of "bargaining" is a fairly common one in many marriages. It is a pattern relating all too often to the sex life of the couple or to other "arrangements" that they make which permit them to avoid asking the important questions about their friendship.

Connie told me that her husband constantly complained about the lack of spontaneity in their sex relationship. She had been advised, for medical reasons, not to take the pill. She found challenge in caring for their three children. She also feared another pregnancy. His "complaining" even included some admission of unfaithfulness. She made the difficult decision to have a tubal ligation to "save the marriage." Her husband left a month or so later. She knows now that he was unfaithful from the first week

of their marriage. She also says, "And, now that I think
about it, I knew that. I was bargaining when I had the
surgery but I had been denying the real problem in our
marriage for a long time."

## Depression

"I'm not a moody person. I have never been depressed
before in my life. I've always been able to deal with my
feelings." Joan was a person who had always succeeded.
Failure had never touched her life in any significant way.
She said there was never anything in her life that she had
wanted that she could not have. Her frustration level now
and the depth of her frustration causing the depression
were in direct proportion to her own former success and
her lifelong feelings of never failing.

People like Ann may heal quicker. She said, "It hurts
that my marriage didn't work. It was my whole life. But
there have been so many things in my life that I wanted
and couldn't have that this is no new experience for me.
Failure has been a part of my whole life. So, I'll try again.
Maybe someday, when I know myself better and am able
to believe in myself more, maybe then a marriage can work
for me."

Frustrated or turned-in feelings are a basis for depression. Often unexpressed anger and hostility produce
profound depression. People sometimes need professional
help in unlocking their complicated and relentless feelings.

## Acceptance

"Two people make a marriage. Part of why our marriage
didn't work was because I had to study all the time to get
through school. I didn't even realize what it was that she

needed from me. . . . Part of why it didn't work was because she didn't tell me that she wasn't happy. I had no idea that she was hurting until I came home one afternoon and found her note on the table telling me that she had moved back to her parents." Now, two years later Jerry is able to admit this. The day it happened he called to tell me that he needed to talk with me, that he couldn't handle the pain, that he wasn't sure that he wanted to go on living.

In one of Arthur Miller's plays, *The Misfits,* Roslyn meets her husband on the steps of the courthouse. He asks her, "Why do we have to be divorced?" Her answer reveals the experience of many when she says, "If I am going to be alone, I want to be alone by myself."

Sometimes it takes a long time for people to realize that for very human reasons they were alone in a marriage. With this realization comes the belief that their decision for divorce, however painful, was courageous and life-giving.

Finally accepting a failed marriage is very important. There are many people who have been divorced for years who are, psychologically, still married. They have not accepted reality.

I met a young man not long ago who said, at a group meeting, "No matter what, I'll always be her husband." Their divorce was final more than a year ago and she is now remarried.

A young woman told me, "It says in the bible, 'Ask and you shall receive.' I am praying for a second chance with my husband and I know that God will give it to me." Her divorce was final more than two years ago. When I explained to her that God will always be with her, giving her strength and inviting her to new life, she said to me, "You don't think I should pray like that, do you? You don't think I should pray for my husband's return, do you?" I explained that to pray is to listen carefully to our own lives and to believe in the invitation to life that God is giving us always. To pray faithfully is to realize that God does not manipulate the life of another to answer our prayers.

The journey through the pain of grief is greatly helped by the presence of others who understand our coping mechanisms, friends who are involved and who are able to stand by us when we are in pain. I am convinced that what the separated and divorced sometimes read as rejection or lack of concern is, in fact, a lack of understanding of grief or an inability to be present to someone who is in pain. Human beings in general are not known for their ability to communicate caring and support when someone is hurting. There is a tendency to either want to remove the pain or to ease it, when what the person needs is our belief that he/she can walk through the pain. What they need is our presence to them in sensitive and gentle ways.

Once we learn that people never "get over" a divorce, that they never let go of the experience of that failed marriage, then we can be present to them without increasing their hurt. To deny what once was, to try to erase five or ten or twenty years of one's life is to become a fractured and disconnected person. To accept the failed marriage as a part of life's growth and the ongoing deepening of the meaning of human life is to face reality. It is to find personal strength and healing.

Nancy asked me, "How long will this pain last? Will I always hurt?" The experiences shared with me by hundreds of divorced people helped me form my words when I said, "It is possible that you will always feel pain when you think of that relationship. So many life associations, even the recurrence of anniversaries, birthdays and holidays are like ongoing reminders of something that once was. But, when that pain is tempered by your own belief that choosing this divorce was an act of faithfulness to

God's call to life, then the pain will have healing qualities like a surgeon's knife that cuts in order to heal."

I have never met a divorced person who went into a marriage expecting to be divorced. And when they realize that it is their marriage and not someone else's that has failed, they are shocked and unbelieving. Whether or not they grow through this initial disbelief and begin to rebuild their lives depends on their own strength and their own faith in their ability to heal. To resist the pain or to deny it is to embitter and destroy the life they still choose.

Out of that initial feeling of shock that "My life, like a shepherd's tent, is struck down and borne away from me," comes the prayer, "My eyes grow weak: O Lord, I am in sadness, be my strength."

Anne Morrow Lindbergh says with great wisdom and insight: "I do not believe that sheer suffering teaches. If suffering alone taught, all the world would be wise, since everyone suffers."

The separated and divorced know well that to suffering must be added grieving, understanding, patience, love and the willingness to open oneself to life again. To heal one must be willing to remain vulnerable—open to the call to life.

# 4. When Does The Annulment Process Heal?

*This, then, is what I pray, kneeling before the Father, from whom every family, whether spiritual or natural takes its name. Out of his infinite goodness, may he give you the strength through his Spirit for your hidden self to grow strong, so that Christ may live in your heart through faith, and then, planted in love and built on love, you will with all the saints have the strength to grasp the breadth and the length, the height and depth, until, knowing the love of Christ, which is beyond all knowledge, you are filled with the goodness of God.*
*Ephesians 3:14-19*

To say the word "annulment" is to speak a Church word, a word that evokes a variety of responses. It is also a word whose meaning is unclear to many who hear it. When I hear the word, I think of the dozens of people who have asked me questions about annulments over the past five years. Sometimes they are parents like Dick's mother whose pain was apparent as she asked, "Do you think there is any chance for my son to get an annulment? He's only 24. His wife left him with their small baby. He doesn't even know where she is. I just can't believe that God expects him to live the rest of his life alone."

Sometimes questions about annulments are asked by people like Janie who told me, "The church is important to me. I don't have remarriage in mind right now, but if I ever do, I want it to be in the church." Sometimes friends call to say, "Tell me about annulments. My neighbor hasn't been coming to church since she was divorced and there are some things she wants to know." Not uncommon is the story of a man like Ralph who said, "Fifteen years ago I asked about an annulment and a priest told me that I couldn't get one. But somebody told me that I should ask you because some things are changing in the church."

When I think of the word "annulment" I think of the people I've helped through the initial steps in the process. Their questions come to mind. But, even more, I think of St. Paul's words, "This, then, is what I pray—that your hidden self may grow strong."

My purpose here is not an academic discussion of the annulment process. Nor is it to provide all the information needed either by the person seeking an annulment or by the pastoral person assisting the petitioner in the process.

Santayana said that "He who does not remember the mistakes of the past is condemned to repeat them." People who go through the painful process of a failed marriage may enter into a second and equally impossible marriage unless some serious efforts are made to examine the causes of the failure.

As I continue to work with the separated and divorced

my personal convictions deepen in the belief that some process of healing, some process of sorting, some process of trying to get inside that failed relationship, some effort to come to understand both self and the other, some understanding of the part that each played in developing the patterns that came to exist in the relationship—all of this is a costly but crucial investment in growing to new life. One cannot simply walk away from a broken marriage and walk into a new life and a new growthful friendship without personal effort. One woman told me, "I never thought I'd ever say this, but I know now that every marriage is two people's marriage—that two people are responsible for the way in which the marriage grows or fails to grow over the years. In the beginning it is so much easier to see what the other person did or didn't do. Now I see my own part more clearly and, however painful it has been, I see my own contribution to the destructive situation that we eventually lived in."

Our lives are always, at once, past, present and future. We need to remember our past and be open to the present so that we will have the courage to choose the future.

For Catholics who have grown up in a church where divorce was nearly denied as a reality and where divorced Catholics were assumed to be unfaithful to their church, there are some questions so much at the heart of the tension between Catholic and divorced that they can perhaps be dealt with only in the church process we call "annulment." To deny this is, I believe from the shared experience of hundreds of divorced Catholics, to deny the sensitivity of the human conscience and its long process of formation.

I am not suggesting that everyone can obtain an annulment. Neither am I suggesting that everyone ought to seek an annulment. There are real circumstances standing between the millions of divorced/remarried Catholics and their church. These include everything from a lack of information to the fact of numbers too large to be dealt with in present tribunal structures. The canon lawyers working in the marriage tribunals are the first to acknowledge these limitations.

The annulment process has been an important way to healing for thousands of divorced Catholics. Time and time again men and women tell me that it was much more important to them than they had ever anticipated, that they really "needed to be right with the church" before they could open themselves fully to the possibility of another relationship in marriage.

The history of the annulment process as it has developed in the church is rooted in a tradition of compassion. The process grew out of a genuine concern for those in failed marriages. This concern was centered in a desire to help people find healing and strength for their lives. It was an effort to help people remain a part of the church. It carried with it an understanding that, unless the person looked seriously at the first marriage, it was all too likely that they might enter into a second equally painful and unsuccessful marriage. It sought to help people ask the difficult questions to prevent their seeking a way out of a difficult marriage too quickly, a decision they might later regret. It reinforced a concern for the ideal of permanence that Jesus made so clear when he said, "What God has joined together, let no human being put asunder."

As the divorce rate has skyrocketed, the church has been put in a position of responding to increased numbers of Catholics seeking annulments. The divorce rates tell us that just as many Roman Catholics get divorced as do people from any other segment or religion or society. Because of its long tradition emphasizing the ideal of permanence, the church is not prepared to deal with the large number of applications for annulments. Marriage tribunals in this country are not adequate to deal with the number of cases they are receiving even though the number of annulments granted has increased significantly in the past 10 years. It is estimated that only 2% of all divorced/remarried Catholics have had their first marriages annulled.

Because the pastoral people working in parishes and tribunals are presented with a challenging and demanding ministry for which they are often not well-prepared, the church's original message of concern, compassion and healing is sometimes lost. Often those seeking annulments feel that the process is not a channel of compassion and healing but rather an obstacle course being administered by seemingly insensitive and judgmental people. I am convinced that what seems like insensitivity instead is a lack of experience or an inability to identify with the pain of the people seeking help. Most of us are not comfortable with others when they are suffering. In our discomfort we either search for some easy words to say or we communicate our own uneasiness with the pain we do not understand. Too often a person who is hurting interprets this uneasiness either as not caring or as a form of rejection.

## What Is an Annulment?

What the process of annulment seeks to establish is that there never was a sacramental marriage. Because two people went through a church service in the presence of a priest or minister does not necessarily mean that this union has all of the important elements needed.

> The effect of a Formal Annulment is to declare that parties are not bound to a specific marital relationship, stating that the marriage in

question was not a binding sacramental union. It is important to understand the meaning of an annulment. The annulment does not deny that a real relationship existed, nor does it imply that the relationship was entered into with ill will or moral fault. Rather, an annulment is a statement by the Church that the relationship fell short of at least one of the elements seen as essential for a binding union. Therefore, the union in question cannot be seen by the Church as a source of continuing marital rights and obligations.[1]

On the basis of the changes in the theology of marriage growing out of the *Constitution on the Church in the Modern World,* Pope Paul's encyclical *Humanae Vitae,* and following the injunction of Pope Pius XII to the canon lawyers to listen carefully to the findings of the behavioral sciences, the grounds for annulment have been expanded. Not only do the separated and divorced need to understand this, but so does the total church community. Unless careful pastoral instruction is done, the increased number of annulments in the American church may give the impression that the church's teaching on the permanence of marriage has changed or has been weakened.

Ten years ago the grounds for annulment were much more limited. Now there are about two dozen grounds for marriage annulment in church law. In the United States, however, an estimated 85% of all the annulments granted are decided on the basis of one of the grounds: psychic irregularity. This broad and general heading of psychological incapacity is looked at from two different perspectives. The first is that of an incapacity to fulfill the promises in marital consent. The second is the incapacity to make an adequately determined decision to marry.

---

[1] Annulment Procedure, Tribunal, Archdiocese of Chicago

It is interesting, though not surprising, because they are often the ones closest to the painful experience of the separated and divorced, that some of the most compassionate people dealing with failed marriages are the canon lawyers working in the tribunals. They are, in many cases, the ones who have assumed leadership in challenging the church to provide better pastoral care for the separated and divorced. They are also the ones who see and give voice to a need for further simplification of annulment procedures if the church is not going to place people in the double bind of demanding that they follow a process, which for practical reasons asks people to put their lives in holding patterns for unreasonable lengths of time. (In some dioceses the annulment process may take up to two years.)

All too often people have the erroneous idea that an annulment is about proving someone right and someone else wrong; that someone needs to be "faulted" in order to obtain an annulment. This is not true. What the church is trying to establish is that for one of many reasons the right to friendship, the right to a meaningful relationship which is one of the factors constituting the marriage, was not present at the time of the marriage. The process is basically one of fact-finding.

Why annul marriages? Why didn't people know a good relationship was not possible? St. Paul says, "We see darkly now . . . but then we shall know even as we are known." None of us know ourselves completely. Even at the end of a lifelong journey, we will not have unfolded the total mystery that each of us is. We come to know ourselves only in relationships. The closer the relationship, the more we are revealed to ourselves and then to another. If we view life as a journey of self-discovery, then we can widen our view of life to include even broken marriages as not necessarily sinful, or careless or displeasing to God, but simply as part of the painful growing stages along a human journey.

When Jesus spoke to us of human freedom in terms of "knowing the truth which will set us free," he gave us another way of looking at our human journeys. We search a long time and only with great difficulty do we discover, inch by inch, the truth of who we are. Discovering that truth invites new choices. It sometimes challenges us to painful decisions that are little understood by others. Jesus' thought parallels that of Paul when he speaks of "our hidden selves growing strong."

## When Do You Apply for an Annulment?

Sometimes people apply for annulments too soon. I think of Janie who came in the day her husband left. In her darkness and confusion, she called saying that she wanted information about an annulment. What Janie really needed was someone to care, someone to help her through the beginning of a long and difficult period of personal healing. As we continued to spend time together, she stopped asking questions about annulments and began to deal seriously with understanding her first relationship. Later on she was able to give it some kind of closure, to put it behind her. Now, two years later, Janie wrote to tell me that her parish priest is going to help her begin the annulment process.

As I have spent time with separated and divorced, I come to recognize some of the signs that tell me that the person has walked a significant way through the pain and is now healing. Most of the signs of healing are related to the basic question of whether the person has begun to deal with his/her own life or whether he/she is still dwelling on the other person's life. Because of the hurt and frustration related to the failure of the marriage, I initially notice continual "blaming." A person may see clearly what the other person did or did not do. A person can identify the failures of the other much more clearly than his/her own. For example, if there is infidelity, seldom is thought given as to why someone began to look outside the relationship for companionship or for emotional and sexual satisfaction. Divorce rates are high among graduate students. Study, poverty, lack of time for the friendship on the part of one person can cause another, even subconsciously, to look for another friend.

When one person grows to a place of letting go of that first marriage, when the person realizes that one person cannot change another's life, and that all that can be done is to deal with one's own life, at that point the person begins to take charge of his/her life. At that point deeper healing can begin. I have seldom worked through a complete annulment with a person without seeing this change happen, the shift from "blaming someone else" to saying, "Two people made our marriage, both of us contributed to its patterns." It is the realization that for both people a "hidden self" was not known well and not understood. It is the realization that only the truth I discover about myself, however painfully, can set me free to love and be loved.

The longer I work with people for whom annulments are important, the more I become convinced that there is something essential, basic and psychologically sound about looking at and learning from a first relationship, whether or not a person ever plans to enter a second marriage. However unclear the message of the church's caring and concern is for people who turn to the church for help, the stories of many people reinforce my convictions. I see the annulment process described in the following poem written by a friend:

## Journey

> I do not know
> where I am going
> until I see
> where I have been
>
> And when I see
> where I have been
> I also see his hand—
> unseen then—
> inviting me where I am.
>
> And I am
> forever on the Way—
> and he . . .
> Is —
> forever . . .[1]

I am not suggesting that seeking an annulment is the only possible way to discover where we are going by looking to see where we have been. I have known some people who applied for an annulment and received a "No." I have known others whose professional counsellors advised them against going back through that first marriage to which they have painfully given closure. I am meeting an increased number of people who cannot and will not apply for an annulment because they believe they were married. They are unwilling to say that they were never married. They believe they had good marriages for several years, and then something happened to their friendship. There is little response that I can make to a person who says, "The church believes us when we say that we are sorry about any other human failing, however serious. We are not asked to prove, with several witnesses, our regret for any other

---

[1] *Journey,* Carolyn McGlone Miller

human choice we have made. Why should this be different?" I have met the children of annulled marriages who
have said to me, "If my mother and dad were never married, what category does the church put me in now?"
These are human questions, signs of pain and confusion in
those who ask. They are questions that invite a concerned
response. These are real circumstances and they deserve
our respect and sensitivity. They speak to us of the real
lives of real people. People who search to understand what
truth it is that will set them free to again look upon themselves not as failures but as good people who did the best
they could. People who were as responsible to their lives as
they were capable of being at a particular time.

Other people are sometimes an important key to the
ways the separated and divorced view themselves. Trying
to understand their stories might give us some insight into
the annulment process as a way for a "hidden self" to heal
and grow strong. It might also widen our understanding of
something that too few people know enough about, and
that is Christian marriage as the church understands it
today.

## What Do Annulments Mean to Those Who Receive Them?

Bill was retired when he came to me to inquire about
an annulment. His first wife had died. Because of pressures on him to find a mother for his children he married
again. From the beginning the marriage was not a happy
one. After many years he realized that she had never committed herself to the marriage. They had neither friendship
nor companionship. I smile when I think of Bill saying to
me, "I don't know if I'll ever marry again. But you know
how it is, a guy gets kind of lonely sometimes. . . ." Bill
did remarry after he received his annulment. He told me

that he was marrying now with a sense of inner peace he had never known before. His wedding was, for me, a very moving experience. He was crying and had difficulty saying his marriage vows—he was so happy—I remember sharing in his joy and that of his lovely wife. I also remember thinking, but what about those who will not be able to get annulments? Are they any less deserving of the happiness of this day?

I think of Carol who began her annulment process as she was planning to remarry. Several weeks later she called to tell me she was postponing the wedding because she was learning so much about herself. As she thought about her first marriage and her part in it, she realized how many important things she had never thought about before. She wanted to be more sure this time.

I met Bev only a few months ago. Her annulment has been accepted by the tribunal. For two years she hesitated. She had not been able to take the second step and put the story of her relationship on paper. She said that she felt something blocking her every time she tried. The second time I saw her we agreed to talk the first relationship through and then put our conversation on paper to send to the tribunal. From the beginning to the end of our few hours together she continually told me how much she was learning about herself. She had expected that she'd talk more about him, but that she had not given enough thought to her part in the relationship. Gradually she began to remember the ways she had not been able to say her feelings, or help him understand what was going on inside of her. As she left my office she said to me, "This time has been so important to me. . . . It has never been so clear to me that there were and still are many important things I need to learn about myself before I ever think about remarrying."

I cannot help but contrast Bev and Carol's stories with that of Sheila who decided to remarry fairly soon after her divorce, and without an annulment. She still had hostile feelings about her first marriage. She had worked to put her first husband through law school, and even worked so he could do postgraduate work. Then he left her and moved to another city, and married another woman. When I saw Sheila shortly after her remarriage, she began to tell me about her husband, about her new job. She said, "He is still in school. I'm just going to work until he is finished with school." I heard from her recently and she is unhappy with his decision to pursue just one more specialized area of study. . . . Perhaps, in the words of the journey poem, she does not see where she is going because she did not take time to see where she had been.

Marianne told me how she had simply signed a paper that her husband had drawn up when he said he was leaving. She agreed to give him the new home both of them had worked to build because "when you love someone you don't argue about money and material things." Now several months later, she was depressed, nervous, not sleeping and frightened. She was angry with him and feeling guilty about her feelings because "I still love him and you don't get angry with someone you love." Marianne now knows that she has much to learn about what it means to love someone, about her own behavior patterns in that relationship. Marianne and I first talked about this because her mother had told her to come and ask me about an annulment. We haven't yet begun work on her annulment but Marianne is learning some important things about herself.

I think of Karen and Jim who remarried without an annulment for his first marriage. Both of them talked to me about the pressures on their marriage. What Karen gradually began to realize was that she felt guilty for marrying a divorced man. She had not asked some important questions. She had not respected her own conscience. She was learning through a long and painful struggle with her marriage relationship that it is not as simple as saying to yourself or having someone else say to you, "Just get married. If you believe that it's okay with God, it'll be all right." True as that statement is, it is equally true that being as sure as we can that "it's all right with God" is not easy to discern. To act from our own convictions is to develop personal integrity and to form our own conscience. Values gradually become our own. The human conscience is formed over a long period of time and re-forming it is neither a quick nor an easy process.

This is the same kind of question that needs careful attentiveness when someone calls me to say, "I'm divorced and remarried. Tell me that it's all right for me to go to communion." I cannot tell people that they can or cannot go to communion. I can spend time with people, helping them understand their faith better, helping them think about their relationship with God, their understanding of their faith and the sacraments, the wider understanding that the church now has of marriage. And, having done all of this, often over a long period of time, the best thing I can hope to do is to help these persons prepare to make decisions that are true to their own informed consciences as they understand their relationship to God—a relationship examined in the light of the values of the gospel.

## The Annulment Process as One Way for a Hidden Self to Grow Strong

As I mentioned earlier, my purpose here is neither to defend nor demand the annulment process. I am not suggesting that it is or can be the only way to new life for the separated and divorced. For some it may be a process where a hidden self does not grow strong, but is further fractured. This realization has challenged the church to make its ministry to the separated and divorced far wider and more inclusive than just the annulment process as a single option for renewed Christian life. Following the removal of the law of automatic excommunication for re-marriage, parish communities are expected to give pastoral care to the divorced/remarried in such a way as to invite their fullest possible participation in parish life, even if this cannot include the reception of the Eucharist.

I wish to restate the belief that some process of heal-ing, some time given to rethinking their part in the failed relationship, is basic and vital to divorced people who take their own lives and their personal happiness seriously.

I do know that the annulment process, begun with a sensitive and caring pastoral person, worked through with the dedicated men and women working in the tribunals, has been a journey through which personal healing and growth were realized in a way not expected or even hoped for. The faith of the separated and divorced, their desire to remain a part of the Catholic community, opens them to the possibility for new life of which St. Paul speaks when he says: "Out of his infinite goodness may he give you the strength through his Spirit for your hidden self to grow strong."

# 5. What Are Some of The Unanswered Questions?

*This means that if anyone is in Christ, he is a new creation. The old order has passed away; now all is new. All this has been done by God, who has reconciled us to himself through Christ and has given to us the ministry of reconciliation. I mean that God, in Christ, was reconciling the world to himself, not counting men's transgressions against them, and that he has entrusted the message of reconciliation to us. This makes us the ambassadors for Christ, God as it were appealing through us.*

*II Corinthians 5:7-20*

"They turned me down. How could they turn me down? After a year and a half, a lot of time, and a lot of pain, they turned me down. What am I supposed to do now?"

This was the beginning of a long conversation with a man named Bill who had just been refused an annulment. With tears in his eyes he talked to me about how much his faith had gradually come to mean to him. He told me that he had never prayed and never had so much feeling about God's presence in his life as he had since his divorce. He said that he had never looked forward to receiving the Eucharist as much as he does now. He knows that the Eucharist never meant so much to him.

He talked to me about his first marriage, about the many ways in which it was, from the beginning, an unhappy and destructive situation for both him and his wife. His four children live with him now. He has met a woman he wants to marry.

After he had applied for his annulment, Bill and his friend began attending a marriage preparation program that was helpful to both of them. It never occurred to either of them that his annulment would be refused. She is Catholic and both of them want to be married in the church.

He talked about the church in a loving way. I have not often heard such care for the church expressed by those wanting to be married in the church for the first time. He spoke of God's importance to their love. He recognized their need of God's help in sustaining their friendship. Both of them know that their church and their faith will be important to them through all the years of their marriage, not just at the time of the marriage ceremony itself.

Since our conversation, Bill's question continues to haunt me. "What am I supposed to do now?" It is a question being asked by thousands of other Roman Catholics who feel rejected by a church that they love. They feel that they are being denied the healing and help that they need and want from a church that is "home" to them.

I am not suggesting that there is or ought to be an easy answer to Bill's question. The question is as complex as are our human feelings and as delicate as is the human conscience. I know of no divorced Catholic who believes that there is a simple solution. Because there is no easy formula to be applied, because individual people do not fit into structural provisions must not mean that there is nothing that the church can do. The message of Jesus' life remains clear. His invitation to new life, to a "seventy times seven" ability to begin again reminds us that Jesus never put people in the position of inviting them to believe that they had no options, no choices. Jesus gave no indication that life allowed us only one mistake and no second opportunity. On the contrary, his invitations to new life are challenging and irrevocable. They are not accompanied by long lists of qualifications. Jesus presents the clear ideal, recognizing that in our humanness we will not always live according to our ideals. Jesus saw the ideal as the highest goal for which we strive. Have we changed that and instead asked the perfection of the ideal as the minimum?

With St. Paul we ask, "How has Christ entrusted his message of reconciliation to us?" What are the implications of this sacred trust for us and for the church? Perhaps nowhere are these questions more challenging and more exacting than in our efforts to be channels of Christ's reconciliation to the separated and divorced. Reconciliation involves finding a meaningful place between the ideal and the possible.

Perhaps we have too often thought of the reconciliation and peace of Jesus as freedom from struggle, as a way without tension. I am reminded of a message from a friend signed, "May the aching, searching, restless peace of Christ be with you always." I have thought of that message often as I continue to meet separated and divorced Catholics who need and want Christ's peace and reconciliation.

I know that in my own life it is precisely in the tension-filled and painful growing edges that I have discovered not only new life and strength but also God's presence. The new life and strength seldom grow out of clear insights and comfortable self-assurance. We struggle to find the passage between "the old order and new" of which St. Paul speaks.

When I think of the married Catholics that I know who have said to me, "In the process of all this work that is being done with the separated and divorced, are you going to destroy something that we believe in? Are you going to destroy marriage?" When we have talked about this, these same people have told me, "It's not easy to be married today. There are so many pressures on marriage. We don't mind having the divorced find healing, but we don't want the ideal of permanent marriage destroyed in the process."

In this statement, they put into words what is, I believe, at the heart of our call to be Christians. At the heart of Christ's message, as we see it lived in his own life, is an invitation to new and stronger life. This life comes not by removing the tension, but by struggling with it and cherishing it as the source of renewed life. Life that comes not by reaching for answers but by searching for the meaning of the questions.

Rainer Maria Rilke, a poet and philosopher, gives important insights into this when he says:

> . . . I want to beg you, as much as I can, dear sir, to be patient toward all this that is unsolved in your heart and to try to LOVE THE QUESTIONS THEMSELVES like locked rooms and

like books that are written in a very foreign tongue. Do not now seek the answers, which cannot be given you because you would not be able to live them. And the point is, to live everything. LIVE the questions now. Perhaps you will then gradually, without noticing it, live along some distant day into the answer . . . .[1]

Jesus' invitation to life and the example of his own life are a reflection of the challenge of Rilke to "love the questions themselves." It is the challenge that is presented to us countless times on the pages of the Documents of the Second Vatican Council where we find the tension revealed between the ideal and the real, the tension between law and life.

Speaking of shared worship in the *Decree on Ecumenism* (n. 8) we read:

Such worship (common) depends chiefly on two principles; it should signify the unity of the Church; it should provide a sharing in the means of grace. The fact that it should signify unity generally rules out common worship. Yet the gaining of a needed grace sometimes commends it.

Speaking further of the implication of shared worship and participation in the Eucharist in the *Decree on Eastern Catholic Churches* (n. 26) we find:

Divine law forbids any common worship which would damage the unity of the Church, or involve formal acceptance of falsehood or the danger of deviation in the faith, of scandal, or of indifferentism. At the same time pastoral expe-

---

[1] *Letters to a Young Poet*, Rainer Maria Rilke (New York: W. W. Norton and Company) pp. 34-35.

rience clearly shows that with respect to our Eastern brethren there should and can be taken into consideration various circumstances affecting individuals, wherein the unity of the Church is not jeopardized nor are intolerable risks involved, but in which salvation itself and the spiritual profit of souls are urgently at issue.

Hence, in view of the special circumstances of time, place, and personage, the Catholic Church has often adopted and now adopts a milder policy, offering to all the means of salvation and an example of charity among Christians through participation in the sacraments. . . .

The council fathers, in their words of concern and in an effort to exclude no one from God's life and grace, give meaning to St. Paul's words that speaks directly to the concern for the separated and divorced in our own time: "All this has been done by God, who has reconciled us to himself through Christ and has given us the ministry of reconciliation."

The council fathers extend the letter of the word of the law to include the uncertain questions which, while they have no easy resolution, must yet be taken seriously. They are questions to which some response must be made by the church and by us.

As the church continues to pursue questions regarding the reception of the Eucharist for people of other traditions many divorced/remarried Catholics are asking why the church sometimes shows greater sensitivity to people who have never been members of the church than it shows to its own members. They question the genuine pastoral concern of a church that has sometimes put the divorced/remarried in a position of not being welcome to receive communion at a wedding, while people of other faiths are, with great sensitivity, invited to "full participation," including receiving communion.

The story of Audrey and Jack is not as uncommon as some might think. Jack was divorced and married Audrey without an annulment. (His marriage could probably be annulled now, but not at the time they were married.) When their oldest son was married, the entire wedding party was invited to participate in the Eucharist— only the bride and groom were Catholic. Jack and Audrey told me how they felt when almost everyone in the church, except themselves, received communion at their son's wedding.

In such situations, it has happened that a divorced, remarried non-Catholic member of the wedding party has been invited to receive communion with the wedding party while a divorced, remarried parent or other member of the family could not.

I am not suggesting that there are simple pastoral solutions to these questions. I am posing the challenge to the church to widen its vision of responsible pastoral care for all. To perpetuate the myth that all divorced, remarried people have rejected their God and their church, or to claim that the difficult choice to remarry is an indication of their choice to reject Christianity, simply does not stand up in the light of the lives of these faithful people.

The questions are as basic as asking what religion is all about. If we view religion and prayer as sources of security, as total tranquillity, as freedom from pain and darkness, then we have understood neither Jesus' life nor his invitation to be the bearers of his message of reconciliation.

The church has been unfaithful to Jesus' invitation to reconcile to the extent that it has attempted to remove tension either by making more laws or by trying to provide

unchanging and all-encompassing answers to difficult questions. Often, before we can be channels of reconciliation
to the separated and divorced, we have to help them rethink the most basic truths of Christianity: Who is God?
What is prayer? What did Jesus mean when he spoke of
the truth as freeing?

Much of the destructiveness of separation and divorce
is, for Roman Catholics, related to the sense of failure and
guilt that they carry because of their own misunderstanding
of who God is and their inability to accept the humanness
that Jesus accepted when "The Word was made flesh and
came to dwell with us." Good people are torn between
what their best human instincts have told them and what
their misconceptions of God and religion continue to tell
them. They view divorce, painful as it is, as a choice to
live more fully Christian and more deeply human lives.
They wonder how God can be displeased with what their
deepest instincts tell them is faithfulness to him and to
themselves.

One source of tension for married and unmarried
Catholics is the annulment process. It is important to be
able to look at the process, to look honestly at its potential
for healing while, at the same time, seeing its limitations.

Married Catholics have, for the most part, as little information about annulments and what they mean as do
the divorced. Because their understanding of marriage is
not well-informed, because they are not aware of the
change in the church's understanding of marriage since the
Second Vatican Council, the married are sometimes confused and sometimes angry with all the talk they are hear-
ing about annulments. A not uncommon question asked
is, "Why can they get out of their marriages? Mine isn't
always easy either." The question shows a lack of understanding of both the annulment process and the trauma of

failed marriage resulting in divorce.

The divorced often begin to learn about the annulment process only after their separation. Sometimes they seek the information. Sometimes they are urged to look into an annulment by a relative or friend. They tend to look upon an annulment, at least initially, as a "church divorce." They often seek annulments as their only way of "staying Catholic." Few know that you cannot make application for an annulment until the divorce is final.

Sometimes divorced people look into the annulment process and, like Phyllis, they turn away sadly saying, "This is not for me. How can I say that I was never married when I had 15 happy years with a man I still love and with our children? As far as I am concerned, I was married and I don't want to prove to someone that I wasn't." The phenomenon of failed marriages poses a whole set of questions different from those related to marriages that the church annuls.

The annulment process offers to some the reconciliation of Christ. For others, annulments are not possible. Some perceive the process to be more hurting than healing. Some attention to the stories of those about whom we have just spoken is important. It may help us understand more deeply that the challenge to the church in our time is to minister to all, to find ways to give all a home. It is a challenge to help those whose lives happen to "fit" present structures, as well as to those in broken marriages or second marriages for whom there is no easily applicable "category."

Often, at the end of days filled with appointments I have, on reflection, realized that almost nothing talked about in my office during that day had anything to do with any readily available answer or any clear way to find new life.

Some time ago I spent a long time on the phone with a young divorced man who has been a Quaker all his life. He wants to marry a Catholic. She readily admits that a church marriage is important to her mainly for her parents' sake. He has received some help from her parish priest who has been open and understanding, but he is having difficulty getting a feeling for the whole annulment process. He said to me, "If this is important to Darlene, then I'll try and do it. But, I don't know much about the Catholic Church. I don't know anything about your laws. I just don't know if I can get a feeling for the annulment process. Is there any other way?" I had to tell him that I don't believe there is any other way that they can be married in a Catholic Church. I don't believe that divorced people can remarry in the church without an annulment . . . I do believe there are other forms of pastoral help that can be given. I do not believe that people are required to live single for the rest of their lives because a previous marriage cannot be annulled. Millions of divorced Catholics are confronted with this difficult question. They feel torn between what they believe is faithfulness to their own lives and a realization of their love for the church.

Annulments are a Catholic solution. One wonders about the whole issue of religious freedom as it is explained in the documents of Vatican II when someone who is not Catholic is expected to enter into the annulment process.

While it is vital that a person come to an understanding of self as well as the dynamic of a failed marriage, it is sometimes psychologically destructive for that person to have to dredge through the details of a first marriage to which satisfactory closure has already been given. Many people wisely seek the help of professional counsellors while they are dealing with the pain of separation and divorce. If this has been done, then either that person or the counsellor may sometimes judge that it would be more hurting than helpful to do all the detailed recall that is necessary in applying for an annulment. As professional people working in the church, I believe that we must give equal respect to other professionals and believe them and their advice. Once again, this presents difficult pastoral alternatives. As Anne said, "I hope to marry again, but my counsellor and I have decided that it is not advisable for me to open the annulment process . . . Is there any way that I can still be Catholic—even if I can't be married in the church?" The removal of the law of excommunication for remarriage puts Anne's question in a new context. But, the difficult pastoral questions of the other sacraments remain.

Sometimes the ease or ability of one person to get an annulment depends on the cooperation of the other person in the marriage. Sometimes that other person says that he/she will never cooperate. Sometimes there is a threat of physical harm if one seeks an annulment. Sometimes this becomes one more way for one person to act out hurt and frustration in the face of an unworkable marriage. I have had people tell me, "I know my testimony is the key. But I am so hurt and angry that I'll never help . . . Marriage in the church isn't that important to me even if it is to her." While tribunals say that a person could receive an annulment without the cooperation of the other person, the nature of some cases is such that the process is either more possible or much simpler with this cooperation. All too often it is the person who needs and wants the church most that feels penalized.

To establish an effective case for an annulment the availability of witnesses is required. With the mobility of our society, many people make application for an annulment to a tribunal that is far from family and friends who could provide the needed information . . . . Telephone and correspondence can help, but there is little doubt that, in the full analysis, distance does interfere at least with the efficiency and the length of time it takes to complete the process.

The church has long had a history of annulling failed marriages where it can prove the marriage was never consummated. As the understanding of marriage has grown these past years greater emphasis has been placed on all aspects of the relationship rather than just sexual expression. In an effort to mirror the love of Christ for his church, the right to friendship in its fullness is the heart of marriage, not just the right to sexual intimacy which is only one part of the relationship. Divorced people who know of this earlier tradition of the church ask, "Why can a failed marriage be granted the assurance of an annulment because it has not been physically consummated when it is clear to both of us that our friendship and our relationship were never consummated in any meaningful way?"

The early church showed a compassion for the very real difficulty that existed in a marriage when one of the two people, after the marriage, chose to become a baptized Christian. The church recognized that the difference in the values of these two people could make it impossible for the person seeking baptism to follow the call to Christianity with faithfulness. As a consequence the church recognized the dissolution of the marriage. In our time, people come to recognize, with great sadness and with a sense of failure, that their differences are too great to be reconciled, that faithfulness to life is not possible in this marriage. Cannot the church today be as creative as the early church was in liberating people from destructive situations and offering them new life and hope?

I talked recently with a canon lawyer who said to me,

"We grant a 'yes' on every application. I believe that the seeds of destruction can be found in the early history of every failed marriage. I believe that there is professional opinion that supports this thesis. So, we grant every annulment for which application is made."

Many would question his opinion, and certainly few tribunals are that clear in their decision-making process. It may be easy to get an annulment in one diocese, while difficult if not impossible in others. This inequality causes pain and confusion in the minds of the separated and divorced as well as among other Catholics. I am not suggesting that the process should, therefore, be done away with. I am suggesting this as a challenge to simplify the process even further. It is also an invitation to search faithfully in response to that tension of which I spoke earlier.

Tribunals tell us that, even with the added efficiency of the American procedural norms being used since 1971, the annulment process has now served less than an estimated 2% of divorced/remarried Catholics. What of the others? In an age when the church has begun to talk seriously again about evangelization, the separated and divorced who love the church continue to ask, "Does this mean that the church cares more for those who aren't Catholic than it does for us?" This same question is raised when they hear invitations to receive the Eucharist being extended to those of other traditions who share our beliefs in the Eucharist.

For all the efforts on the part of the tribunals to be equitable, there can be little doubt that aggressive people who call the tribunal to inquire about the progress of their case often receive more prompt and effective action than a less aggressive or a fearful person might receive. One woman told me that in the more than four months since her case had been mailed to the tribunal, she had received no word. She said, "I am afraid to call for fear that they might not like it and that would interfere with my getting an annulment at all." This tells us something of the apprehension with which many people approach the process.

The attentiveness to detail and the efficiency of the pastoral person to whom the divorced person goes for initial help also contribute to the acceptance of and favorable decision in a case. Many pastoral people have not refreshed their own understanding of marriage and of canon law. They are simply not capable of giving the help that is often needed. Certainly the separated and divorced cannot be expected to have all the information that helps make the process more effective, however well-intentioned they might be. In contrast with the woman I mentioned, I know of another person who called the tribunal every week. That case came through significantly faster than other cases coming out of that same tribunal.

There is a vast difference in tribunal judges. As with the judges in our civil courts, their interpretation of the law is filtered through their own understanding of the law, an understanding related to their own personal experience and personal approach to law. It is clear that we cannot praise the humanness of the church when it is to our advantage and then condemn it when it is not. At the same time, when people are hurting and when their whole future seems to depend on a human channel, these very human differences can easily appear as barriers between them and their church. The differences can also obscure their understanding of Jesus' message of reconciliation. They question the inequality of interpretation they find in the "ambassadors for Christ."

It would seem fair to say that the emphasis of the church on the annulment process has tended to obscure other kinds of pastoral care that are also authorized and sanctioned by the church. One often gets the impression that to speak of what the church calls the internal forum solution (the priest dealing with the individual's conscience in individual circumstances) is somehow suspect or irresponsible.

Certainly dealing with the long-formed conscience of adults is a delicate process. It is a process which requires a high investment, first of all, in developing an understanding of the process of conscience formation and then in the time spent with an individual person. But, to speak of all of this is a very different thing from the kinds of seemingly ominous warnings given, as though every person who mentions internal forum were either giving people "easy answers" or somehow finding loopholes far removed from acceptable pastoral care.

Father John Finnegan, in an article called *Spiritual Direction for the Catholic Divorced and Remarried,* says that there are some important guidelines for a priest or pastoral person who counsels people in relation to "internal forum solutions." Urging an adequate knowledge of contemporary theology and a sound sense of the delicacy of the human conscience, Father Finnegan says:

> He should inculcate a reverence for the teaching authority of the Church, and be certain that personal decisions of conscience respect the Christian value of permanence in marriage. The priest (pastoral person) can never ask people to make a moral decision that they are unable to make and one which does not support what they fully believe. The pastoral person never counsels people in disobedience. He presides over a process . . . he tests it, directs it, seasons it with gospel values, and insures that what is taking place is growth in maturity and love of Christ and His Church.

The sensitivity required in using the internal forum process cannot be overemphasized. It is a challenging and often time-consuming endeavor. When pastoral people seek too easily to replace an old conscience with a new one, when one set of answers is replaced by another, the result can only be destructive. The key for responsible ministry in this regard is helping people discover their own beliefs, their own values and then examining these values in the light of gospel values. Counsellors sometimes seek to replace what they believe to be an "out-of-date conscience" with their own "more advanced and far-seeing conscience" without going through the long process of informing, clarifying, judging and making one's own, whatever set of values one chooses as a frame of reference.

People often say to me, "I'm divorced and remarried. Can I go to communion?" Or, "I'm divorced and I want to get married. Will you find a priest who will marry me?" The answers to either of these questions do not rest with me. The answers, or at best sometimes, the decision made, must be based on the individual person's own understanding of their stance before God and in relation to their understanding of the healing they need and want from the church.

And so the unanswered questions remain. They remain not as problems to be solved and not as invitations to more laws or to simple answers. Life and strength reside someplace between St. Paul's challenge to us to be healing "ambassadors for Christ" and Rainer Maria Rilke's challenge "to be patient to all that is unsolved and to love even the difficult questions." If we share this search for life, realizing that the unanswered questions are like wellsprings of creative energy, we will discover new life. Struggling with the questions can make of us the ambassadors of Christ who communicate his message of healing.

# 6. How Do The Divorced View Marriage?

*A faithful friend is a sturdy shelter; when we find
a friend we find a treasure. A faithful friend is
beyond price, no sum can balance the worth of
that friend. A faithful friend is a life-saving
remedy.*

*Sirach 6:14-16*

"With all the divorced people you meet, with all the
experiences they have shared, with all the pain and hurt
that come in the wake of a divorce, do you still believe in
marriage? Do divorced people believe in marriage?"

The young man who asked these questions is not
married. He is searching for the meaning of friendship in
his own life, struggling to understand the demands of faithfulness and commitment. He does this in a community of

friends, many of whom have shared with him their hurt and discouragement following a divorce.

As I paused a moment before responding to his questions, I thought of the many others who have asked those same questions. I was reminded of a book I read called *Should Anyone Say Forever?* I spoke to him out of convictions that continue to deepen as I work with and share life with the married and the unmarried, as well as with the separated and divorced.

My answer is clear. More than ever I believe in marriage. I believe that marriage is possible. I have been convinced of this, to a large extent, by the separated and divorced who have helped me to understand what Christian marriage means and what it asks. Marriage is a journey that encompasses two important aspects of life: shared friendship and gradual self-discovery. Understanding what each of these means and what it asks is at once challenging and life-giving. The vision and the courage needed are found in a willingness to respond to the invitation of an ever-present and ever-loving God to reflect on the meaning of our human lives in the light of the values set out clearly in the life of the human Jesus.

My reflections on the aspects of shared friendship and self-discovery began when I asked some divorced people to answer the question, "How Do You View Marriage?" The following pages are their response:


Marriage, as I pictured it back there in the pre-Cambrian period around 1947, would be a warm cocoon. I would be his wife. We would have fat, rosy-cheeked babies, would dine by candlelight, would be each other's one and only, or in my mother's old-fashioned phrase, each other's "hon and dearie." When his spoken fantasies penetrated my daydreams, he vowed success in two of his specialties, sports and politics. We seemed to have pre-fab notions, needing only each other's presence to complete the artist's sketch. It was not point and counterpoint. It was two separate snatches of tune. We did not know it then. Three years of "courtship" and 27 years of marriage—we know it now.

Marriages are not made in heaven. They are built on earth by people with the raw material of initial attraction, verbal felicity, a sense of each's humor, integrity, sexuality—*Value*. They are heaven-blessed in the formal sense sometimes, but I do not now believe that the formal marriage ceremony is as important as the sense of care and tenderness and, yes, excitement in each other's company that day-to-day commitment requires. Which is not to ignore God's help but only to say God is necessary to the entire journey, not just at the embarkation point.

It seems strange to find oneself on the shady side of 40, separated and alone. Not lonely—at least not always lonely. Busy, trying to make up for "lost time"? Perhaps not. No time is lost if you have learned something. Even painful lessons are part of one's private evolution. Strange, and somehow exhilarating.

Marriage is a daydream no longer. Which is not to say I do not think of it as an ideal state. I have lowered my expectations. Were I to have the opportunity I would expect more—and less —at the same time. I'd expect less of all the material things I once thought were necessities. I'd settle for stainless, would not have to worry about babies anymore. Candles are still gracious dining accessories, but good food, lovingly prepared (by either party) seems important now. The days and hours and minutes now are important to "husband"—in the cherished sense of that word. It is important that the minutes count, the words not hurt, it is important that the hands that reach are able to touch. I'm so much wiser now. I know so much about loving, from not having been so good at it for so very long.

I see two people in their 70's walking down Brattle Street every morning as I walk to work. I wonder what it's like to grow old loving someone "to death" 'til death. Good marriages are worth the building, but they are not solo flights of fancy. How rueful to discover this, how lucky to realize it—even now!

—**E.M.**

\*     \*     \*

To me, as a person who has been separated almost three years and divorced two years, as a Catholic whose annulment has been received, marriage is the choice of a relationship I want to have. To me, marriage is the most satisfying relationship, the most appropriate, the most comfortable commitment I've observed. I write "observed" because I do not feel that I ever experienced a true marital relationship. I had a facade of marriage for almost 20 years—a facade so destructive to myself and to my former spouse that my choices were separation, suicide or insanity.

Since my separation I have worked hard to change myself. Changing and growing is dreadfully hard work. If I cannot grow to be the sort of equal partner I want to be and if I do not find the type of partner who wants an equal relationship, then I will not marry again. I need to be able to give and receive love, friendship and affection, but my esteem of marriage and my recollection of the trauma of divorce are such that I do not want that experience again in my life. My paper marriage did not lack financial security; it was rather an experience of emotional poverty.

What I have from my paper marriage is an experience I wish never to repeat in another adult relationship. I now have insights into my strengths, resources and faults. I have a better relationship with my children. I have learned to put my faith and my feelings first and my finances last in my priorities. I have learned compassion and caring. I have had some wonderful persons and events enter my life. Since my separation I have made the break with the facade and have started to become me.

I believe that marriage is the ideal relationship for adult men and women.

**—M.G.**

\*     \*     \*

I believe marriage is a "setting"—a setting for living, loving, caring, sharing, being, touching, and, ultimately, growing with each other, toward each other, toward God.

Marriage, a true marriage, has no limits. It grows like a "Love Ball" until it expands, touching all in its path and, in turn, lending growth.

Marriage is real. It lives in the mind, heart and spirit. It is an attitude shared by two.

Marriage is a communication on all levels, an understanding that "clogged lines" need not remain so.

Marriage is a commitment to spouse and to God. We are in each other's hands—both in God's hands.

Marriage is elevated friendship toward a favorite companion—a bona fide PAL.

Marriage is a long and arduous walk—taken step by step—with pauses along the way. Pauses for rethinking, rechoosing both the direction and the pace.

Marriage is also a willingness to sometimes let the branch veer, with freedom, still part of the one tree.

Someday I'll be married again—correction—someday I'll be married.

**—P.M.D.**

\*　　\*　　\*

Marriage is sharing life intimately with a special person. It is making a commitment to another person, yet not suffocating and stifling that person with your love. It is giving and receiving . . . . It is being yourself, without taking the other for granted. Marriage is making mistakes and growing through them together.

**—J.M.**

\*　　\*　　\*

My thoughts on marriage are the same now as on the day I first married my husband. I still feel that marriage is the greatest union between a man and a woman. It needs God's grace and life to continue and to survive through all the pitfalls of life. It is the commitment of one man and one woman for life.

Marriage is the greatest community of love and life where both can grow, where both can give love in a relationship. This cannot happen unless two people live this lifestyle and reinforce it with trust, respect, faithfulness, a belief in God and in each other.

**—L. O'D.**

\*　　\*　　\*

## A Celibate Reflects on Marriage

Can we who never married say a word about what marriage is? I believe that we can. Priests and religious in our church believe in marriage and are continually sobered and challenged by this vocation. Husband and wife and children—sharing, loving, and living are in a human situation filled with countless invitations to Christian excellence. They share relationships captured by the writers of sacred scripture that bespeak God's love for us and Christ's love for the church.

To nurture and care for marriage as a priest is to watch over the symbol of God's love for me and the church. I see myself as a priest called by the church to protect all the symbols that talk to us about God. Serving and upbuilding marriage and family life is not only a rich human experience for me, but it is also a way of ensuring that my beloved church has a way of contextualizing and expressing God's love in simple human language.

**—Father J.T.F.**

## Marriage As Shared Friendship

"Thus the man and woman, who are no longer two, but one flesh" (Mt 19,6), give mutual help and service to each other by their marriage partnership, through which they become conscious of their unity and experience it more deeply with each passing day. The intimate union of marriage, as a mutual giving of two persons, and the good of the children demand total fidelity from the spouses and require an unbreakable unity between them.[1]

---

[1] *Gaudium et Spes*, Sec. 48

This paragraph taken from a document of Vatican II, like the reflections of the divorced, speak to us of sharing and growing together as friends. We know that neither sharing nor growing happens automatically. Sharing and growing are choices we make. There are skills we need, and barriers we discover sometimes only with great difficulty.

I once gave a series of retreats for couples which I called *Marriage: A Commitment to Friendship*. Present at those weekends were people not yet married and people who had shared as many as 28 years of marriage. The universal response to the theme was, "It makes so much sense. But, no one ever told us this before. No one has ever talked seriously to us before about friendship in marriage. No one has helped us deal with some of the basic ideas about what friendship means and how you grow to be friends."

I also learned of the widespread fear in the community of married people that to spend a weekend retreat together was to give some signal to others that a marriage was "in trouble." We will not turn divorce rates for Catholics around until we help the not-yet-married and the already married understand that the journey in shared friendship and self-discovery needs continual and ongoing investment. This journey demands a belief in the importance of prayer, understanding and dealing with feelings, listening skills, respect for differences, the realization that we need a community of friends who share our values, and a willingness to see all of this as a part of each person's pilgrimage to ongoing life.

## Our Failure to Understand Christian Friendship

Friendship, like many of the other things that we take for granted as a part of our lives, may be one of the "givens" we understand least. It may be something that we have failed to reflect on in such a way as to be able to give ourselves to a relationship and allow the other person to give the self that he or she is.

We live with confused myths and with sometimes superficial impressions of love and friendship. While human feelings enrich and give beauty to our lives, there is a choice dimension to faithful friendship that serves as an unchanging support even in the presence of our sometimes fitful and changing feelings. In *The Brothers Karamazov,* Dostoevsky says of love and friendship: "Love in action is a harsh and dreadful thing compared to love in dreams."

The questions of the young man who asked me if I believe in marriage led us into a long discussion about friendship as a necessary part of personal growth without which good marriages are not possible. We discovered that there are cultural and societal preventatives that sometimes interfere with our ability to deepen our insights into the meaning of friendship, especially friendship between men and women.

*In our society there is a destructive and very early "coupling effect."* Even young children do not escape it. This coupling effect puts unrealistic pressures on teenagers which they are often ill-equipped to deal with. It often propels people of an age for marriage towards marriage in the reverse order. They become lovers first, married second, and then, if ever, discover if they have enough in common to be lifelong and committed friends. Someone has said that "too many people get married." Marriage has been assumed to be the only path to personal and psychological wholeness for men and women. Removal of the societal and cultural pressures may be the only route to discovering what marriage means in terms of full Christian life.

Most of the world assumes that deep and lasting relationships between men and women will, either at the beginning or at some point, lead to marriage. This assumption has deprived us of a fuller understanding of human relationships in general, and those between men and women in particular.

*Despite the fact that there has probably never been so much talk about sex, sexual experience, and sexual liberation, the truth is that our understanding of human sexuality is both inadequate and incomplete.* There has been an emphasis on the physical dimensions of sexuality that has largely excluded the integrating and relationship dimensions of sexuality. Our sexuality is so much at the heart of who we are as persons that it touches on all that we do. The creative force of our sexuality may be in its power to unify the human personality. Only when we understand human sexuality better will we be able to see it in a context of being one important aspect of human friendship rather than viewing it—as is too often the case now—as either the only or the most important factor in friendship.

*The different ways in which men and women have been culturally trained to deal with and express feelings is one of the greatest obstacles to their sharing friendship.* Generally, tough feelings have been more acceptable in men, both in experience and in expression. Very little boys were told (and sometimes continue to be told), "Be a man, don't cry," "Be strong like your dad," "Don't let anyone know when you are hurting, it's not manly," and a host of other equally destructive notions. Women lived with a feeling of acceptability in relation to tender feelings. It was expected that little girls (and big girls, too) would cry, would manifest hurt feelings, would need protection, would tell others when they hurt. We live now in a crucial time when sensitive men and women are realizing a shared need and a common responsibility to liberate our human feelings so that sharing friendship and life are more possible and mutually life-giving.

*The fear of intimacy, the reluctance to risk the cost of sharing life and human experience with another person, touches on all of the other factors that we have mentioned.* Herbert Hendin, in his book *The Age of Sensation,* voices a concern based on his research through the end of the 50's, through the 60's and into the 70's. He is concerned with the cultural patterns and social practices that may help to destroy experiencing the human intimacy necessary for meaningful and enriching human relationships.

Because we live in society and are surrounded by the patterns of secular culture, our ability to evaluate our human experience in relation to Christian values is made more difficult. St. John tells us, "No one has ever seen God. Yet if we love one another God dwells in us and his love is brought to fullness in us" (I John 4:12). Our human relationships, our personal investment in faithful friendship is at once the threefold key to loving and caring for ourselves, to being able to enter into loving and caring relationship with another, and to finding the link between ourselves and God who is the source and center of all love and friendship. To the extent that these four factors influence us—to that extent shared friendship, which is at the heart of Christian marriage, is not possible.

## Marriage as Gradual Self-Discovery

In his introduction to Ernesto Cardenal's book *To Live Is to Love,* Thomas Merton says:

> . . . In order to attain such a mature act of love, we must first have experienced contradiction and

conflict. Love is the pinnacle of freedom and of a fully personalized consciousness. And love discovers its own being only in the act of love. A love that acts without being fully conscious of its action, acts contrary to its very nature and does not attain to a full consciousness of self. It remains, as it were, in hiding before itself. . . .

And what shall we say of this kind of love? That it should not be? That it is sinful? That it should not be permitted or should be punished? Alas, it is surely true that our poor love tastes of sin. However, Ernesto Cardenal says of it simply that it is LOVE, but a love that is not yet sufficiently free, not yet sufficiently pure. And we might add that by what it lacks in being true love we may discover the way that leads to true and perfect love. It is by ACCEPTING THIS IMPERFECT LOVE, FULLY CONSCIOUS OF ITS IMPER-FECTION, THAT OUR LOVE MAY BE MADE PERFECT.[1]

Thomas Merton, in reflecting on Cardenal's work, is reminding us of something that we already know. We learn to love only by trying to love; we come to a place of faithful and liberating friendship only by continually searching for the meaning of friendship. As we do this, we gradually discover who we are and we determine who we want to be.

The message of the Christian gospel makes it clear that we do not grow to full human life except in relation-ship with others who share both our search and our values. Each of us has a lifetime journey through which we come to know ourselves more fully through our experiences and in relation to the people with whom we share these ex-

---

[1]*To Live Is to Love,* Ernesto Cardenal (Doubleday Image Book) pp. 12-13.

periences. It is in our personal and shared reflection on these experiences that we find both meaning and vision. It is in the act of sharing that we find direction for our lives.

Gustav Thibon in one of his books says that "the love of another person creates nothing in us, but that love sets free all that is already there." The growing places for self-knowledge emerge at the places of intersection between human lives. We know ourselves in some ways, and that knowledge, when linked with the image of ourselves, is reflected to us through others, helps sustain the self-discovery process.

When we consciously or subconsciously choose to distance ourselves from other persons, we may be choosing a way that will be much less painful, but we are also choosing a way that prevents our becoming a person who has enough self-knowledge to enter into sustained and sustaining friendships. To choose to avoid human closeness in friendship is to choose to close doors on life that can only be discovered in human relationships.

Rainer Maria Rilke describes human life as a room in which each of us lives. He says that most of us get to know only a small part of that room because we continue to choose to stay in the familiar and secure part of that room that we know. Only to the extent that we are willing to explore the unknown areas of that room do we become more fully human and more fully Christian.

Another way to express Rilke's thought might be to ask ourselves what kind and size room we want to live in. If we choose the security of the smallest room, we also choose the limitation on life and loving that necessarily accompanies such a choice. We may not hurt as much, and we may not hurt others as much. But, we will also never love or be loved as much.

It is important for the separated and divorced to relate

their pain and sense of failure to the human journey they
share in common with every other person. As human
beings we live in the darkness, insecurity, lack of experience, and lack of insight that are a part of being human.
We need to understand this as a part of being human rather
than as a part of being failures as human beings.

Gregory Baum in his book *Journeys* says, "We realize
that we cannot come to self-knowledge by looking at ourselves; only as we are engaged in conversation with others,
and reflect on their reactions to us, are we able to gain
greater insight into who we are."

Some people enter into marriage with a knowledge of
self and an understanding of marriage that are important
factors in sustaining a committed, lifelong friendship.
Others, for a variety of reasons, come to a deeper understanding of both, only by growing through the painful
process of separation and divorce. Thomas Merton's words
seem so filled with insight: "What shall we say of this kind
of love? That it should not be? That it is sinful?" What
shall we say of these lives? Of this painful experience?
We cannot say that it "should not be permitted." We must
say that "It is by accepting this imperfect love, fully conscious of its imperfection, that our love may be made
perfect."

We need to remember that the painful journey
through a failed friendship is not an automatic dispenser
of a deeper understanding of friendship, nor is it necessarily a revealer of self. The fact of the failure of the
second marriages of so many of the divorced is clear
evidence of this.

There is a high personal price on both friendship
and self-knowledge. The separated and divorced are learning that the support and caring of others who share their
experience can be an important support for growing

through a divorce to new life. They are also realizing that preparation for a second marriage is important—a preparation they may be able to enter into with a kind of personal openness and with a sense of need for preparation that was not a part of and probably not possible at the time of their first marriage.

### What Do the Divorced Tell Us of Marriage?

Marriage is like a tapestry that two people weave together. Each person brings the materials and color of self. The tapestry is one, but the threads are separate. When two people who chose to join their lives now begin to separate their lives, when this tapestry is torn apart, there is no way to measure or describe the pain. The decision is made with some realization that the tapestry no longer depicts a journey in friendship—a journey shared and cherished.

In Arthur Miller's play, *The Misfits,* Roslyn meets her husband on the steps of the courthouse. He says to her, "Why a divorce?" Her response is like the experience of others who painfully discover that they are no longer friends. Roslyn says, "Why a divorce? If I am going to be alone, I want to be alone by myself."

Through years of either not experiencing friendship or not knowing how to be friends, the separated and divorced long for the kind of friendship described in Sirach: "A faithful friend is a sturdy shelter, a treasure, a life-saving remedy. . . ."

# 7. What Do The Divorced Want from The Church?

*You were strangers to the covenant and its
promise; you were without hope and without
God in the world. But now in Christ Jesus you
who once were far off have been brought near
through the blood of Christ. It is he who is our
peace, and who made the two of us one by
breaking down the barrier of hostility that kept
us apart. In his own flesh he abolished the law
with its commands and precepts, to create in
himself one new man from us who had been two
and to make peace, reconciling both of us to
God in one body through the cross, which put
enmity to death. He came and "announced the
good news of peace to you who were far off, and
to those who were near"; through him we both
have access in one Spirit to the Father. This
means that you are strangers and aliens no
longer.*

*Ephesians 2:12-19*

As I continue to work with the separated and divorced
I am often asked, "But what do they want? What are they

asking for?" It is sometimes not easy to put words around the answer to that question. Finding the answer might be like the difficulty we have in answering the questions we ask of family and friends when we try to deepen our understanding of the bonds we share. At the heart of relationships are sets of feelings—feelings that often defy being framed in words. It might be like asking a black person to say simply how it is to be black and to tell us what black people want from us.

I received an important insight into the question of what the divorced want from the church when I gave a talk and two workshops at a conference in a large city. Because of a scheduling problem we had joined the parish community for our closing liturgy. We had gone to the Eucharist wearing the tags that marked us as participants in "A Day for the Separated and Divorced." As I was leaving the church after the Eucharist a woman from the parish, seeing my conference tag, approached me saying: "I know all about you divorced people. Why should I have to go to Mass with you? What right does a woman like you have to go to communion? You people who destroy your own marriages so you can just live careless lives have a lot of nerve coming into our parish to destroy marriage for those of us who believe in it." She didn't give me an opportunity to respond, though I am not sure I would have tried. She pushed me aside and walked out of the church ahead of me.

I think of the first meeting we had with the separated and divorced Catholics group in a parish where I was working. When the notice was put into our parish bulletin, I received a call from an angry lady saying to me, "I am shocked. You are a Roman Catholic Sister. Don't you believe in marriage? What are you doing letting those people meet in our buildings?"

I also think of a neighboring pastor who told the

separated and divorced in his parish, "You go there for your meetings. I don't want this kind of radical, far-out thing going on in my parish."

While these incidents speak to us about what the divorced sometimes have not had, but what they need and want, St. Paul shows a depth of feeling and insight in his clear portrayal of the Christian message: ". . . In Christ Jesus you who were once far off have been brought near through the blood of Christ. It is he who is our peace . . . breaking down the barrier of hostility that once kept us apart."

I consider it a tragedy and an unfortunate loss of opportunity for the entire Christian community that little or no instruction was done in most parishes following Pope Paul's November 1977 statement of the removal of the American law of automatic excommunication for those divorced who had remarried without a church annulment. Sensitivity to the separated and divorced on the part of the total community could have grown and deepened, had time been taken to review the original meaning of this law with its destructive misinterpretation over so many years, and with the implication of its removal. Reviewing this impact on the families and friends of the separated and divorced, as well as on the divorced themselves, could have been healing. Few people ever understood the meaning of the law. This lack of clarity has alienated millions of divorced Catholics from both their families and their church.

I met a man recently who had not gone to communion in 15 years. In the confusion, like thousands of other divorced Catholics who have not remarried, he thought that to be divorced meant to be "out of the church." He believed that because he is divorced he is no longer welcome to participate fully in the life of the church. He had no accurate information about either the law of excommunication or its removal.

After a talk in a large city, a woman approached me with tears in her eyes. She said, "I am so happy that I am here tonight. My son is being confirmed next Sunday. I have been divorced for three years. I have not remarried. In all that time I have gone to Mass every Sunday but thought I could not receive communion because I am divorced. Do you understand what it means to me to know that I can receive communion on my son's confirmation day? If I hadn't come tonight, I would not have known that."

For so long good people have lived with destructive misunderstandings of an 1884 law. There was never a time when this law of excommunication applied to the divorced. There was never a time when divorce prevented a person's taking communion. The law applied only to the divorced/remarried.

An article that I read in a newspaper quoted Dolores Curran who had read Bishop Cletus O'Donnell's statement made on behalf of the American bishops. It was the bishops' response to Pope Paul's removal of the 1884 law of excommunication. She said, "What a beautiful pastoral statement. But I worry about the divorced members of the church. Are we in the pews ready to open our arms and our hearts to the divorced among us?"

She went on to say that during her participation in the Detroit Call to Action she has been shocked to learn that some parishes will not let children "from broken homes" be altar boys, will not allow the divorced to be lectors or serve on parish councils or teach CCD classes. She closed by saying that she hoped that "we laity can carry our responsibility in our parishes as the bishops did in the church. Let's ask our separated and divorced how we can help them feel at home in our parishes."

In the recent past I have met couples from Marriage Encounter at five out of six talks given in cities in two states. They have spoken with me after each talk, explaining that they want to know how they might be helpful in sensitizing the wider church community to the needs of the separated and divorced. They also spoke of wanting to give their own help and support. They seemed to understand St. Paul's words to the Corinthians: "I mean that God in Christ was reconciling the world to himself, not counting our transgressions against us, and that he has entrusted the message of reconciliation to us" (II Cor 5:19).

As I reflect on the important question, "What do the separated and divorced want from the church?" I see clearly that there is a wider, deeper and more fundamental question that demands our attention. "What does every person want and need from the church?" If we took that question seriously then we would not have a broken community. We would not have a community in which people, because of their own hurts or confusion or need for healing, respond in anger when Christ's compassion is extended to others. Many of the painful questions that the separated and divorced ask grow out of hurts much more encompassing than their broken marriages. Like many other Christians they are fearful and threatened because they have never really understood well who God is, what the church is, or what marriage is. They have never received the message of Christianity in such a way as to be able to relate it to their own human lives. They have not learned to relate the meaning of Christianity to their own personal experience. Few Roman Catholics even know of, much less understand, the implications of the profound changes in the church's present understanding of marriage.

A demanding challenge to the church today is to

bring the message of Christianity alive in such a way that we could say to every person in the church, "This means that we are strangers and aliens no longer." It means that we are no longer plagued with images of God that separate us from both the love he came to give us and from those we are called to love. It means that we no longer experience ourselves as dismembered and torn inside because we understand that it is in our human experience that God is revealed to us. It means that we can begin to carry our own responsibility for what the church is and what it will be because we see the church as a home shared by the human family as it searches for the meaning of life in the message of the Gospel. It means that divorce rates will only be different if we link the sacredness of marriage and the sacredness of the person in the basic call to committed human friendship—a friendship rooted in the invitation of our baptism as Christians. A friendship deepened by the message of Christ's love and concern for his church.

Let's reflect on these three questions: Who is God? What is the Church? What is marriage? Let's look at those questions with a sense of our personal history reflected in where we have been, where we think we are and where we would like to be in our understanding of the implications of the questions.

It is important to begin with what we have understood. It is important for us to see where we have been because, unless we do, we cannot understand where we are and we may never find the courage to choose the place we would like to be. Without some sense of history, we are a fractured and disconnected people. Without this sense of history, without a feeling for growth and development and change as normal and healthy, we may be agents of destruction in a church we love. I think again of my friend's poem in which she says, "I do not know where I am going until I see where I have been. And when I see where I have been, I also see God's hand, unseen then . . . ."

St. Paul says so clearly that we are God's messengers bringing healing to one another. Our failure to understand who God is and what the church was meant to be has prevented our experience of community even in the church—the one place we most need and hope to find it in today's world.

## Who Is God?

One gets the impression that someone, very long ago, decided that if we spoke of God as love, people might take advantage, people might take the easy way, they might rationalize or make excuses. And so we created a false God. We created an image of a God that is, perhaps, the very image we are warned against in the commandment that says, "I am the Lord your God. You shall not set strange Gods before me." "Setting strange Gods" means putting a god in place of God.

Recently I said to a group of people at a series on religion, "When I say the word 'God,' tell me the first words that come to your mind." We filled the blackboard with words like fear, commandments, hell, punishment, far away, someone who rewards me when I do good, hard to talk to, someone who turns away from me when I sin. . . . We have set false gods in the place of the God who said to us, "This is the sign that I am giving for all ages to come, of the covenant between me and you and every living creature with you. I set my rainbow in the clouds to serve as a sign of the covenant between me and the earth" (Genesis 9:12, 13).

Jesus, who called himself the Way to the Father, told us so plainly, "Love has no room for fear; rather, perfect love casts out all fear" (I John 4:18). Jesus spoke of it in an image that we all understand when he said, "In my Father's house there are many dwelling places . . . I am indeed going to prepare a place for you, and then I shall come back to take you with me, that where I am you also may be" (John 14:2, 3).

We need to take seriously God's ever-present invitation to life. We need to believe the message of the covenant, never broken by God because of anything that we do. God does not turn from us ever. We may choose to walk away from God. We may choose to ignore his persistent presence with us, but the love God gives does not change because of anything that we do or are. God will never cut us off from life and love. Only we can do that.

When I can repeat my invitation, "When I say the word 'God,' tell me what comes to your mind," and know that I will hear, "Love, acceptance, understanding, knows what it means for us to be human, cares for me no matter how often I fail, doesn't count my mistakes, always gives me more than one chance, gave us Jesus to help us understand our own human journey, blesses me with new life when I have failed," when these and other words replace the ones we have known, then we will know that we have an understanding of God and a relationship with God that is faithful to his own promise of faithfulness to us.

The images of God that are still too common among us have made of us an externalized people. God might well say of us, "These people honor me with their lips, but their hearts are far from me." We count on the things we do more than on the kind of people we are to establish bonds between us and God.

Very often the separated and divorced feel guilty at the time they experience their greatest need of God's love. They are afraid that they have failed God and in failing

him have cut themselves off from their source of renewed
life and strength. They fear this even as they say, "But, I
know I did the best I could." They share this feeling with
all their Christian brothers and sisters who envision a
punishing God who invites them to feel bad about themselves instead of seeing themselves as good people, loved
and accepted by God. They have not been told often
enough that God is pleased with them for having been as
faithful to their own lives as they knew how to be. They
have not been told that they are pleasing to God when they
struggle with the meaning and direction of their lives.

Perhaps what the separated and divorced and all of us
struggle with is the image of God that we have created for
ourselves. It is an image that flows out of an understanding
of God that may have been communicated to us, but, much
more significantly, it is an image of God related to our own
personal sense of failure and fear. It may be a projection of
our own insecurity and inadequacy. In the very act of looking for God and his presence in our lives, we are responding to his call to life.

### What Is the Church?

Our mistaken understanding of who God is is related
to our inability to understand what the church is and what
it was meant to be. Often there is little in our understanding of the church that tells us it had its beginning in that
first small community of believers who called themselves
"The Followers of the Way." There is too little that reflects
the vision of Christianity as Jesus lived it in companionship
with all who searched to find the God of Abraham, Isaac
and Jacob, the God of Journey, of Laughter and of Struggle.

We need to remind ourselves often that, as Christians,
our call is not to settle into some meaningless image of the

church. We are called by Jesus to be a people always on the way. As Bishop Carroll Dozier said so well, "We are not the originators of the Christian vision, nor are we its curators. We are called to live the vision as disciples." We are called to live that vision as pilgrims who look for meaning in our human journey.

Teilhard de Chardin, a Jesuit priest and prophet, often spoke of the way in which we have so narrowed the vision of Christianity that many are forced to go away from the church, saddened by their need to look in other places for a vision of life that is adequate. We have so restricted the message of Christ's compassion that many seek healing in other religious traditions. They seek healing in humanistic groups that promise no belief in the existence of a God. They look for strength in groups that do not tell of a God whose faithfulness to us is recorded in the story of a people who most of the time in their history were unfaithful to his promise of life. They seek healing in groups which cannot promise, "It is He who is our peace . . . breaking down the barrier of hostility that kept us apart."

In *The Pastoral Constitution on the Church in the Modern World,* the Fathers of Vatican Council II speak of a tradition of understanding the Church that is more faithful to the message of Jesus in his relationship with his early community of believers:

> The joys and hopes, and griefs and anxieties of the men and women of this age, especially those who are poor or in any way afflicted, these too are the joys and hopes, the griefs and anxieties of the followers of Christ. Indeed, nothing genuinely human fails to raise an echo in their hearts. For theirs is a community composed of men and women. United in Christ, they are led by the Spirit in their journey to the kingdom of their Father and they have welcomed the news of

salvation which is meant for every man and woman. That is why this community realized that it is truly human and intimately linked with mankind and its history.[1]

An understanding of this description of the church would bring healing to those who have been called "strangers to the covenant."

## What Is Marriage?

With the staggering divorce rates (as high among Catholics as among other segments of society) many married Catholics feel threatened and afraid. Many separated and divorced Catholics share with them the question: "Are good and lasting marriages possible?" These questions have challenged the church to take more seriously its responsibility to Christian marriage, a responsibility much more encompassing than simply marrying people. Karl Barth, a noted Swiss theologian, has criticized the church for having had no theology of marriage, only a theology of the wedding ceremony and of the first night.

Few Catholics know that there is a gradually growing and more meaningful understanding of marriage emerging in the church. It is stated briefly but profoundly in the Vatican II document, *The Pastoral Constitution on the Church in the Modern World*. It is also stated in Pope Paul's encyclical, *Humanae Vitae*. In these documents, which served as a basis for the deepening understanding of marriage, is found the basis for the church's more serious ministry to marriage.

This growing understanding of marriage reflects the best not only of the Christian tradition, but also of an ever-

---

[1] *Gaudium et Spes* (Par. 1)

evolving understanding of the human person and of human sexuality. It is an understanding that can give hope and healing to the separated and divorced, new insight to those preparing for marriage, and greater support and enrichment to the already married.

*The Pastoral Constitution on the Church in the Modern World* speaks of marriage in a way that reflects the beauty and goodness of marriage when it says:

> The biblical word of God several times urges the betrothed and the married to nourish and develop their wedlock by pure conjugal love and undivided affection. . . . This love is an eminently human one since it is directed from one person to another through an affection of the will. It involves the good of the whole person. . . .

> Such love, merging the human with the divine, leads the spouses to a free and mutual gift of themselves, a gift proving itself with gentle affection and by deed. Such love pervades the whole of their lives. Indeed, by its generous activity it grows better and grows greater. . . . This love is uniquely expressed and perfected through the marital act. The actions within marriage by which the couple are united intimately and chastely are noble and worthy ones. Expressed in a manner which is truly human, these actions signify and promote the mutual self-giving by which spouses enrich each other with a joyful and a thankful will.[1]

The changes in the Church's understanding of marriage as reflected in the above passages, and the implications of these changes, center around four basic areas:

*Marriage is viewed as a covenant rather than a contract.* Contracts are agreements that are spelled out and

---

[1] *Gaudium et Spes,* p. 48-52

specified. Contracts are agreements about what will be given and what received, and are related to a strict justice system. They deal with the externals and with things. A covenant is related to internal qualities. A covenant is a commitment to unconditional giving. In a covenant there is no measuring of what is given, no limit to what one is willing to invest personally. A covenant reflects God's own promise to care for us, to forgive us, and to love us always.

*The pledge of mutual love constitutes the marriage.* In our former understanding of marriage, the love was taken for granted. Now we understand that the human love constitutes the sacrament. The sacrament is a sign of Christ's faithful love for the church. The presence of mutual love and the ability to sustain a loving friendship are not always easily discerned.

*Belief in God and of his presence in a marriage is necessary for the sacrament of marriage.* There is a serious theological question about whether or not there is a sacrament of marriage unless those marrying accept their marriage as a visible sign of Christ's love for the church. Christian marriage is a covenant through which God's grace is received when it is chosen by two baptized believers.

*The bond that links two people in a marriage grows throughout the marriage.* This means that people grow more married as they continue to choose their shared commitment. It also means that the consummation of a marriage is much more than a biological act, and that sustaining a marriage requires continual personal investment and mutual enrichment.

These changes in our understanding of marriage demand explanation and clarification for all. They also place heavy responsibility on the church to provide adequate pastoral care for marriage in all phases: preparation for marriage, marriage itself, and the help needed in the sustaining of good marriages.

Separated and divorced Catholics share with their married friends a frightening realization that they understood too little about marriage when they married. Like the married, they have not been given adequate information about the church's present understanding of marriage. They are expected to respond to an unexplained and unclear ideal.

While the separated and divorced share the same faith search and the same need as other Catholics to rethink many things that they have been taught, there are some things that they want from the church that others do not need in the same way.

A lady named Marcie told me, "I never realized how important the Church and my faith were to me until I was divorced. Now I look to the church for community, for healing, for compassion in ways I never did before."

A 24-year-old man heard about the divorced Catholic groups in the city where he lives. He called me to ask if he could attend the meetings even though he didn't live in that part of the city. He said, "I dropped out of the church halfway through college. Now that I am divorced, I am hurting and I don't know how to help myself. When I heard that someone in the church cared about the divorced I couldn't believe it at first. If the church is interested in me now, I think I could be interested in the church again."

Separated and divorced Catholics all over the country have been a bridge back into the church for many who left the church at some point in their lives either because they had not experienced the church as a community of believers who bring Christ's love and healing to one another, or because they received the message that they were no longer welcome. Too often the church, instead of reconciling, had condoned alienation. One might ask the important question, "Why are so many people, who look upon themselves as good Christians, so righteous and so judgmental of the lives of others?" Why is it that the same people who condemn the divorced by quoting the passage from scripture that begins, "What God has joined together . . ."—why have these same people not taken just as seriously the injunction of Jesus when he says, "Judge not . . ."?

What do the divorced want from the church? They want the assurance that the love they have for the church is not questioned. They want to be free of the stereotypes that make them marked people in too many parish communities. They want to be able to share fully in the community of believers, sharing, as others do, both their gifts and their brokenness.

What do the divorced want from the church? They want the kind of acceptance that Jesus gave to the woman at Jacob's well. In the efforts of the community to open itself to the separated and divorced we sometimes confuse acceptance and approval. The divorced are not seeking approval for a failed marriage which may have been a place of hurt and destructiveness for themselves and others, any more than Jesus approved of the many marriages of the Samaritan woman. The acceptance of the people who came to him was Jesus' way of bringing healing and a new sense of self-acceptance into their lives. He invites us to do as he did, so that Paul's words become ours:

> Now in Christ Jesus you who once were far off have been brought near through the blood of Christ. It is he who is our peace, and who made the two into one by breaking down the barrier of hostility that kept us apart. . . . This means that you are strangers and aliens no longer.

# 8. What Do The Divorced Bring to The Church?

> *There is cause for rejoicing here. You may have a time to suffer the distress of many trials; but this is so that your faith, which is more precious than the passing splendor of fire-tried gold, may by its genuineness lead to praise, glory and honor when Jesus Christ appears. . . . Come to him, a living stone, rejected by men and women but approved, nonetheless, and precious in God's eyes. You are living stones, built as an edifice of the spirit, into a holy people, offering spiritual gifts to God through Jesus Christ. . . . A stone which the builders rejected that became a cornerstone.*
>
> *I Peter 1:6, 2:4-5, 7*

Great literature and simple folklore, through all the ages, have reflected the hopeful and mysterious theme of great strength and vision emerging from unnoticed and

unexpected places. The sense of our own fragile humanness, and our awareness of the impact on us when people
in high places have left us disillusioned, quickens in us the
need for a place to put our belief that each of us is at once
stronger and more vulnerable than we know. It was this
promise of new and richer life that was the beginning of the
restless searching for the ancient mythic figures of Greece
as well as for the prophets and kings we meet on the pages
of the Old Testament. It is the surprise dimension at the
heart of life that is reflected in words we remember having
been said of Jesus, "Is this not the carpenter's son?"

One of the most powerful scenes in Leonard Bernstein's *Mass* comes at the end when a shattered and per-
plexed community is called to life by a young boy who
moves quietly and undramatically through the lonely
crowd. He reaches out to touch the people around him and
soon they are doing that for each other. In that very act,
they begin to share again and to care for one another. Who
would have expected such healing and strength in one so
young?

In our time in the church we are experiencing the
emergence of the new place of the separated and divorced.
We are witnessing a growing understanding of their important role in the church. St. Paul's words, "There is a
cause for rejoicing here," are reinforced by the growing
conviction in the separated and divorced themselves that
their need for healing and for a home in the church, that
their image as wounded and hurting is being replaced with
a belief in their strength and faithfulness as Christians.

These "living stones," who have known the pain of
misunderstanding, failure and rejection in both society and
in their church, are one important key to our renewed
understanding of both the church and its sacred sacraments. It is a part of the Christian paradox that the very

people who have introduced into the church some of the most difficult pastoral questions—arising out of the tension between upholding the ideal of permanence in marriage while upholding the ideal of the church as the channel of compassion and healing for human lives—are the same people who remain faithful ministers to a church they love. Growing ministry not *to* the separated and divorced but *by* the separated and divorced may be the cornerstone for the church in its ministry to marriage. Out of the painful "splendor of fire-tried gold," the human experience of failed marriages ministered to by a compassionate Christian community, may be the channel of the Spirit leading marriage to new vitality and to deeper faith commitment.

Like the young boy in the Bernstein *Mass,* the separated and divorced, in reaching out for healing, have healed one another. As "living stones" they bring a new vision to the church.

Working full time with the separated and divorced has given me an entrance into the lives of thousands of people whose willingness to invest in their own healing and to share that experience with others has revitalized my understanding of community. My own transition to this work meant leaving a parish community I felt very much a part of. It meant moving to a new city in a new part of the country. It meant searching for a new community of friends.

These changes found me struggling with my own sense of loss, my own feeling of uprootedness, my experience of not yet belonging. I have never known such personal darkness and pain. During those weeks of transition I often thought about the many workshops I had done for the separated and divorced on "Personal Growth: Dealing with the Pain." It was as though I were being called to relate to my own words, not on a theoretical basis, but in a very real way. I struggled to find meaning in the whole awful experience. It was God inviting me to take my own words seriously. I was being challenged to deepen my own understanding of the personal pain that accompanies the separation from or the loss of relationships that nurture life and strength.

During those weeks of transition I was invited to give a talk to a divorced Catholic group in a nearby city. The members of that group were affirming and healing. They were for me a tangible link between a community that I had left and one which I was seeking.

A short time after that talk I received a call from Mary. She said, "I know Thanksgiving is a long way off. I spent my first Thanksgiving alone last year. If there is any chance that you are going to be alone on that day, come here to spend the day with me and my family. I don't want you alone on that day like I was."

This lovely lady, so sensitive to me and to the darkness I was experiencing, brought tears to my eyes with her thoughtful invitation. This lady, so fragile, too, was hospitalized just a short time later for severe depression. Even in her own darkness, she could care about me and with such sensitivity be a channel of healing for me. As I look back now, I realize that her invitation was the beginning of my own gradual process of feeling my life coming together again, of feeling at home in my new surroundings.

The painful uprooting experience just described has left a deep impression on me. During that time of transition I was aware that, even on the darkest days, I was doing something that I had chosen. I knew that it was a decision that I had made over several months. It was a decision made with personal prayer and with loving support from friends. When I questioned my decision, I remember asking myself the question again, "How do people come through the awful experience of separation and divorce? What is it that keeps them from falling apart, even physically?"

As I ask that question, I know that I have met hundreds of divorced people who, like Mary, in the midst of their own pain still find the time and strength to be agents of healing for others.

When I think about the question "What do the separated and divorced bring to the church?" I think of three particular gifts that they have given to me. These gifts are like three doors that have been opened. I believe that they are also gifts to the total church. These three gifts are: first, a richer understanding of the meaning of compassion; second, a more inspired sense of ministry; and third, an invitation to deepen our understanding of each of the sacraments.

### An Attitude of Compassion

I recall a poignant scene from the film, *A Tale of Two Cities*. In the midst of the terrible suffering in France at the time of the revolution, an old man is found hidden away in an attic. He is an aristocrat who has lost everything. He portrays a gentleness even toward his enemies that is mysterious to his questioners. He responds with a wisdom that I have thought about often. He says, "In the midst of great pain and suffering we learn many things. But the most important thing we learn is the lesson of never bringing pain into the lives of others."

Millions of separated and divorced Catholics have experienced the trauma of the failure of a marriage they cherished and to which they were committed for life. They are confronted with the added pain that comes from their

own feeling that they have failed themselves and God.
Often they are judged and rejected by righteous people
who say too easily, "Good Catholics don't get divorced."
And yet, they continue to love the church and to seek a
home there. They want to find in the church a place where
they receive Christ's healing and his promise of life.

Their continued presence in the church, even in the
face of rejection, speaks of their own deep faith and their
great love for the church. It speaks of their gentle patience
with a church that has seemed unresponsive to their pain.
It speaks of their courageous hope that someday they will
receive from the church what they need and want—healing
and acceptance.

Once again, we find in God's Word a meaningful expression reflecting the response of the separated and
divorced to the church:

> The Lord answered me and said: Write down
> the vision clearly upon the tablets, so that one
> can read it readily. For the vision still has its
> time, presses on to fulfillment, and will not dis-
> appoint; if it delays, wait for it, it will surely
> come, it will not be late. The impatient person
> has no vision; but the faithful person will live.[1]

## A Sense of Ministry

During the five years that I was in parish ministry, the
one question that the parish council and the staff continued to ask was, "How can we get our people involved
in people-to-people ministry? How can we take this parish
of 1800 families and make the links between those who
have a particular need at a particular time and those who

---

[1] Habakuk 2:2-4

could minister to that need?"

As I continue to work with establishing support groups for the separated and divorced, I realize that this is exactly what is being done. It is being done so effectively and so extensively that it could well serve as a model for the entire church.

I think of Marcie who told me about the group she had started for teenagers whose parents were separated. She said so simply, "I have teenagers of my own. I know that my divorce was hard on them and I don't always know what to do for them. Maybe if the teenagers start getting together they could help each other." She told me that she began by putting a notice in her parish bulletin and in the local newspaper. She said, "I provide lots of pizza and a place for them to meet. We'll see where it goes and decide what we need to do as time goes along." In three years that group has been a place for healing the pain of children whose lives threaten to be broken by a broken marriage.

I smile at, but am also amazed by, the story of a lady who started what may be the first "Travelling Divorced Catholics Group." This ingenious person had gotten together a small group of divorced people who held meetings in various parishes in the area where she lived. She talked to each pastor, arranged for a meeting place and then came in with her small divorced Catholic group to meet with the separated and divorced in each parish. Her efforts had been very successful. The groups were growing. Some were established and no longer needed her help. This generous woman brought her own gift and helped others find theirs.

I was in the Midwest recently for meetings in several different cities. The meetings were arranged by a man who says that because a group helped heal him he now wants to help others establish support groups.

There is something about the shared experience of pain that breaks down the barriers that separate people. The experience is not unlike the stories told about the "good old days" in a suburb that was leveled by a tornado 15 years ago. Whenever groups of people in that community come together, it is inevitable that, at some point, there will be talk of the tornado and of how people came to know their neighbors for the first time. Never before or since, they say, have they experienced that same sense of caring and community.

Several editions of a local newspaper were used to recount stories of the response to New England's Blizzard of '78. In the wake of that catastrophe, people were attentive to and responded to the needs of others in ways at once unusual and healing. In times of crisis, we cut through our patterns of separation from one another.

There is much said and written today in the church about "wounded healers." There is a growing sense among people in churches and in the helping professions that they first need to recognize their own brokenness, their own wounds, in order to be able to be compassionate to another person. Without this realization, much of what is called "ministry" or "healing" is, in fact, only the multiplication of acts of either condescension or oppression. Acts of givers who have not learned to receive may destroy and harm instead of building and healing.

People dealing with the needs of the oppressed and the poor in the Third World tell us that the first step, and a key for those who wish to work with the oppressed, is to identify, own and acknowledge their own needs as well as the ways in which they are at once oppressed and capable of oppressing others.

Compassion is a gift that is basic to ministry. It is brought to the church in much the same way as St. Paul speaks of it. It is a gift brought by those who know well their own brokenness, their own hurts and needs. It is a gift brought by those who realize that they have hurt others. It is a gift brought by those who realize that we are all "members of Christ's body."

The compassion brought by "wounded healers" such as the separated and divorced, is a gift that enriches a church in need of its own healing. The second important gift of which we have spoken is the gift of patience. It is a gift that has kept the separated and divorced in the church when they might have left in discouragement. It is a gift that they share with us as they teach us about ministry and caring.

I think of a woman in her late sixties who told me, "For more than 30 years I have continued to go to church, but always feeling like a black sheep in my parish. . . . I've lived with the hope that someday I could again feel at home in my parish. I know that God loves and accepts me, but I need to feel that the people I sit with at Mass feel that way. . . . It's been so long. . . ."

One of the tremendous lessons I have learned from the separated and divorced is that they are patient with the church in ways that many of us sometimes are not. They seem to have an ability to accept the humanness of the church, an ability to wait for its healing, in ways that many other members of the church community do not. Any small signs of hope and compassion go a long way toward their healing and toward their willingness to heal others.

A woman who lives in a parish where the pastor has forbidden the divorced Catholic group to meet told me, with great gentleness, that she "understood," that as long as she knew there were parishes where pastors were not only permitting but encouraging the formation of support groups, she could continue to believe and to wait.

## The Challenge to a Deeper Understanding of the Sacraments

We have spoken about the sensitivity and compassion of people who have struggled with their own lives and come through that struggle with renewed life and a greater understanding of the struggles of others. Surely this is the richness of the lives of "living stones, built as an edifice of the spirit, into a holy people offering gifts to God."

We have talked about the ways that the separated and divorced have helped us to understand better what it means to live in community, what it means to help one another and to heal one another.

Though the separated and divorced would probably not think of it like this, I am convinced that they offer to us some important keys to deepen our personal understanding of the meaning of each of the sacraments. Their experience of pain and failure is so profound as to touch on every element of personal life. Their sharing of that experience with me has given me some new insights into the meaning of the sacraments in my own life. Their experience offers new insights into the meaning of the sacraments for the lives of all Christians.

## Baptism as the Sacrament of Community

For many Catholics, baptism still carries with it associations only of "removing original sin," of making the soul "acceptable to God" in a way that it once was not. For many, it is not a sacrament that is thought about in any meaningful way. It is often looked upon as something "done to me" when I was a baby, something that made me a member of the church. If any or all of these ideas about baptism reflect the deepest understanding a person has, that person is being deprived of the ongoing support of community and of the deeper meaning of all the other sacraments.

The separated and divorced, in their painful experience of broken lives and in their need for support and friendship if they are ever to be healed, reach out to one another in an understanding of the importance of community that is at the heart of our baptism as Christians.

We are baptized into a community. We are invited to share life with other members of that community. The promise of baptism is that life and the ability to sustain our commitment to Christianity are only possible in the presence of others who choose to live with the ideals of the gospel. It is a promise that members will so cherish those ideals and try to live them and others will be inspired and strengthened in their efforts to live them.

The challenge of baptism is for that same community to provide healing to broken marriages while, at the same time, providing strength and support for the married. In denying a place to the divorced in our communities for fear of weakening the ideal of lasting marriage, we have so weakened our total community that we have not been able to provide adequate enrichment and strength for the married.

The value of the permanence of marriage, like any other ideal given to us by Jesus, will not find its support and strength in society in general. Every ideal that Jesus gave to us borders on the countercultural in such a way as to necessitate our finding others with whom we share these ideals if we hope to make them meaningful in our lives.

The separated and divorced, in coming together in support groups, are a reminder to the total Church to take more seriously our commitment to baptism as an ongoing sacrament. They remind us that faithfulness to the values of Jesus is linked with faithfulness to a search for the meaning of community.

## Reconciliation as the Sacrament of Ongoing Healing for Community

When we have experienced our own failures, when we have not realized the ideals that are ours, when we question our own ability to be faithful to ourselves and others, then we understand our need for healing in a way that we never can when we succeed.

When we have done the best that we could, when we have invested as much of ourselves as we understand, when we have sought for help beyond ourselves and have still not reached some goal, then we search for a strength that is larger than we are.

When we have reached out to others for help and been rejected, when even those closest to us seem to be saying that we are not acceptable because we somehow do not measure up, when we are even told that God is displeased with us for not having done what we could not do, then we will either find some new place to reach to or withdraw from for fear of further hurt.

Reconciliation is a sacrament that threatens to be lost to the church. It is a sacrament that, like the others, has not been understood because until now it has not been rooted in meaningful form, and because we have so misunderstood both who God is and what sin is. We have not found ways to help the Christian community experience reconciliation as a sacrament of healing for their lives. We have been deprived of the experience of healthy guilt because we have induced so much unhealthy guilt.

The separated and divorced, in their experience of

the deepest kind of human pain they have ever known, reach back into the church community to find healing for their lives. They are a living invitation to understand this healing sacrament in a more truly Christian, more deeply human way.

### The Eucharist as Food for the Weary, As Bread for the Journey

The stories of divorced and remarried Catholics who have continued to come to Sunday Mass through 15, 20 and more years without receiving the Eucharist are much too numerous to recount. This does not reduce the personal pain in each of those stories.

Equally painful is the realization of the thousands of divorced Catholics who stopped going to communion because they thought they were excommunicated by the fact of their divorce.

Unless this pain is to be valueless for the wider community, we are faced with the challenge of deepening our understanding of the Eucharist. We are given an invitation to go back to the time of Jesus, to his life and to his own understanding of the Eucharist and to see what this is saying to us today.

With the added emphasis in church teaching on the incompleteness of the "Mass without communion" because of the renewed understanding of the Eucharist as a meal to be shared, we have removed the understanding we once had of communion as some sort of reward for good behavior with the implication that only the "worthy" could approach the sacred table. Popes condemned the old "O Lord I am not worthy" theology because it placed people in the position of never daring to approach the Eucharist. It is clear that receiving the Eucharist, as it was given by

Jesus, was never a question of "worthiness" for him. Jesus spent so much time and shared so many meals with the members of that early community that were judged to be sinful by others, that some judged Jesus to be a "glutton and a sinner."

The questions about receiving the Eucharist must rest with Jesus' own understanding of his own words when he said, "When you do this, remember me . . ." and "This is my body given for you. . . ."

At the same time, it is important to recognize that the questions we ask in the effort to discern Jesus' understanding of the Eucharist are asked in the context of history and in the context of a church community that has deep-seated, even if unclear, patterns of thought and understanding about requirements for the reception of the Eucharist. It is important that responsive ministry to one group of people in the church not happen at unnecessary cost to another group.

Much of the theology of the church, of Eucharist, and of community as it is reflected through the documents of Vatican II places us again in the uncomfortable tension of exploring wider perceptions of the community that may be, while not sacrificing the ideals of the community that is.

**Marriage as the Sacrament of Friendship**

Perhaps one of the greatest gifts that those in failed marriages bring to the Church is their insight into marriage itself. Human beings seem to learn from what did not work as well as from what does. Separated and divorced people who chose marriage as their way of life, who valued its commitment and permanence, hold some of the most valuable experience and information in relation to marriage—information and experience that they often ask to share with those preparing for marriage and with the married in need of continual enrichment.

It is not uncommon for marriage preparation programs in the parish to include the separated and divorced on the team. More parish education programs, taking seriously the challenge of the meaning of the high divorce rates, are searching to find new ways to give support and enrichment to the married.

Separated and divorced Catholics know well that the ideal of commitment to Christian friendship in marriage is as demanding and personally costly as it is life-giving and rewarding. The married live in social groups where the values of Jesus are so little thought about as to not be a source of questions. But, the separated and divorced, who have taken seriously their own ongoing call to life, have struggled to understand their own lives. Out of the ruins of a failed marriage they often come to know themselves well enough to view the prospect of another marriage as a response to God's call to faithfulness to life. Those who have cared enough about their own lives to search for the meaning of the failed marriage are investing with greater security in a commitment to the meaning of marriage for others.

The presence of the divorced in society and in our churches has been so misunderstood and so threatening that we have not learned from the sacred experience of their growth through great difficulty and personal pain. The divorced, more than anyone else, in their faithfulness to God's call to life have been faithfully persistent in challenging us to listen carefully and to take seriously the experience they have been willing to share.

Our understanding of human friendship and our realization of our need for human relationships are being "fire-tried." The faithfulness of the divorced to their church invites our commitment to search together to find ways to prepare for, to tend and to mend marriages.

There is a cause for rejoicing here. At a time when divorce rates have never been higher, we may be coming closer than ever before to what is at the heart of the sacrament of marriage. Through the painful searching process, we may emerge as a Christian people who, for the first time, have an insight into what St. Paul meant when he spoke of the love of the two people in a marriage as a mirror of Jesus' love for the church.

## What Do the Divorced Bring to the Church?

In the face of what once seemed insurmountable obstacles, the divorced now give to their church a sense of compassion that arises only out of the personal experience of one's own need for compassion and the fear that it might not be given.

The "living stones" who have known rejection, bring a sense of the costly caring that is at the heart of ministry to others. They bring a conviction that the signs of human meaning are present in the sacraments of a church they love.

# 9. How Do The Divorced Reveal The Meaning of The Mystery of Human Suffering?

*Always, wherever we may be, we carry with us in our body the death of Jesus, so that the life of Jesus, too, may always be seen in us. Indeed, while we are still alive, we experience death every day, for the sake of Jesus, so that in our mortal flesh the life of Jesus, too, may be openly shown. So death and life are at work in us.*

*But as we have the same spirit of faith that is mentioned in scripture, "I believed, and therefore I spoke," we too believe and therefore we too speak, knowing that he who raised the Lord Jesus to life will raise us with Jesus in our turn, and put us side by side in his presence.*

*II Corinthians 4:10-14*

In his meaningful and perceptive way, Neil Diamond, in a song called *Come Dry Your Eyes Now* speaks of Jesus as "that distant, fallen angel that descended much too soon." And then, with great depth of insight and in a way that nudges one with the reality of life he says, "He taught us more about giving than we ever cared to know, but, we've come to learn the secret and we'll never let it go. . . ."

Not only has Jesus "taught us more about *giving* than we ever cared to know," there is a way in which we could say that our lives challenge us to experience more of *living* than we sometimes want to know. More than we want to know about loving, about caring, about forgiving, about accepting ourselves and others, about any of the ideals presented clearly to us in the call we have received to live as Christians.

In every invitation to *live* and to *give* is the ever-present and costly mystery of pain and death, the mystery of human suffering.

Pain and suffering are a part of that same "secret" and we'll never let it go, nor will it let go of us. We journey in the companionship of "life and death, blessing and curse" says the book of Deuteronomy. The question then is not whether or not suffering will be a part of our journey. The question is what sort of companionship we will choose to have. The question is what meaning we will find in our companionship with suffering. The question is how we will allow the mystery of suffering to reveal itself to us.

Human beings have wrestled with the meaning of suffering through all of recorded history. Job has become the classic figure who did not travel easily in the companionship of pain. Many other stories are recorded of people who suffered and cursed God as well as people who suffered and, in the end, blessed that same God.

We often ask the question, "*Why* do we suffer?" That question does not seem as important as the question "*How* do we suffer?" It seems that to continue to ask the question *why* is to put our energy into a channel that may not lead us far. It may be to put our energy into eventually being angry and cursing God. Suffering is a reality of human life. It arises from social structures as well as from each person's darkness and human frailty. (This is not to say that we ought not invest in fighting against evil and the harm done by sinful structures and persons.)

The question I want to deal with here is the *how* of suffering . . . the way we walk with suffering . . . the way we find our own growing edges through its presence in our lives.

I want to clarify why I have spoken of the "mystery" of suffering and what I mean by mystery. Our catechisms taught us to define a mystery as "something that we could not fully understand." That very definition means that we took everything from basic mysteries of faith like the Incarnation or the Trinity, to the mystery that each person is, and locked them into some sort of unexplored holding pattern. This definition excused us from looking deeper at these fundamental realities.

I want to define mystery as something so knowable, so self-revealing, so illuminating that we will never succeed in penetrating the depth of all the meaning that is continually being revealed to us. There is too much meaning for us to comprehend at any given time.

The meaning of the mystery of human suffering was revealed to me recently in my meeting with Tom. He came into my office apologizing for not having called to make an appointment and asking for information about the nearest divorced Catholic group in the city to which he would soon be moving. Two hours later, we were still talking. . . . I did not tell him then, though one day I will, how moved and frightened I was to think that one man could have absorbed so much pain in less than a year. Tom reminded me of so many things I believe—that we are all stronger than we know, that we all have hidden reservoirs of power in us that work for us when we need them. I believe that God's love and strength are revealed to us through our human experience of nearly dying, nearly not continuing the journey with so fearsome a companion as pain. I also believe that it is only in retrospect that we realize what suffering means. Soren Kierkegaard says, as though the lines had been written of human suffering, "We live our lives forward, but we understand them backwards."

I did tell Tom that I was aware of a goodness and gentleness in him, a living embodiment of precious "gold that has been tempered and tried by fire." I did tell him that I had met others who had not seemed to have suffered as much who were embittered and paralyzed by their own resistance and anger in the face of their pain. Something in them had rejected the companionship of suffering.

In less than a year Tom had experienced separation from a wife he still loves, leaving his home and moving away from his children who are important to his life, the death of a nephew to whom he was very close, the loss of a financially rewarding job which made it necessary for him to move from his home in the suburbs to a single and unfurnished room, the inability to find work over several months, a call to the deathbed of his mother which he almost did not receive because he had no phone and just happened to be in his room where a policeman contacted him, the death of his mother, and now, having finally found a job, the need to move to a distant city, away from his children.

This gentle, beautiful man, often with tears in his eyes, spoke of what the nightmare of the past months had been for him. He described his feelings of loneliness and desolation. He spoke of coming close to suicidal despair.

As I listened to him I wondered if I have his faith and strength and courage. I wondered if this pain would have found me asking, "*Why* do I suffer?" rather than "*How* am I suffering? What meaning am I finding for my life? What strength is being revealed in me through this?" I wondered if I could do as Tom had done or if Neil Diamond's words would be true of me, "He taught us more about giving than we ever cared to know." Whatever pain I could still see in Tom's face, it was clear to me that he had captured some of the meaning of the mystery of his own suffering.

Tom's gentleness reminded me of a tiny, sensitive woman I met at a recent conference for the separated and divorced. She was sitting in the front row during a talk I gave and I noticed her immediately. Not only was her expression one of love and affirmation for me, but I saw, especially, the gentle lines in her face—lines that spoke of suffering and pain that had been channels of life and love. When I talked with her later she told me that she was 73, one year divorced, a divorce she did not and still does not want. Her pain was very near the surface of her life and her tears were shared with some embarrassment for her. As I was leaving that meeting, someone pressed something into my hand and did not stop to speak. She had given me her name tag on which she had written, "I love you. . . . I need you. . . . Please pray for me. . . ."

These two stories, like thousands of others, are reminders of God's strength and life, reminders that "he who raised the Lord Jesus to life will bring us to life with Jesus" if we, like Tom and this lovely lady, can find a way to ask not *why* but *how*.

Several years ago, in the pain of the renewal period in religious communities, a friend gave me a wood and pewter plaque she had made. The words on that plaque reflect her sensitive love for me. They also give voice to the universal experience of suffering:

> Like blind men and women we grope in a world
> of textures, afraid to touch the jagged edges of
> life. But those who reach out to embrace them
> find that the same jagged edges that have pierced
> them have also made them whole.

The story of every separation and divorce, like the story of every difficult human decision leading us into the unknown, is an unfolding of a journey entered into in the companionship of darkness and pain. There is no easy way to separate out human lives that have been linked, whether in friendship in marriage or apart from it. There is no fear-free way to enter into an unknown future. There is no certitude that any decision is life-giving in every respect. At the heart of the human decisions made at some turning point in life is the realization that this decision could be for us the best or the worst. There is an ever-growing sense that we do carry with us at once the death of Jesus and his life.

Suffering invites each of us to enter more deeply into our lives, it challenges us to go beyond the question *why,* beyond the question *how much.* It calls us to ask the question *how,* to search for the meaning of suffering in such a way that we will not settle down in some form of self-pity or of measuring our pain against what we believe to be someone else's pain. Suffering is a mysterious invitation to embrace those jagged edges that both hurt and heal.

As I have continued to search for the meaning of pain and suffering in my own life and as I have shared that same process with others, it seems to me that we have some built-in barriers to embracing those jagged edges. We measure carefully our willingness to journey with pain. Some of the barriers reflect a society that looks for quick and easy ways to remove or deny pain in whatever form it comes to us. Some of the barriers emerge out of religious backgrounds that have confused the meaning of suffering in such a way as to intensify its pain and rob us of our strength. There are many such barriers. I want to reflect on a few that seem most significant to me because of their implications. They are:

1. A subtle but persistent "Who has sinned?" mentality.
2. The fallacy that God loves us most when we suffer.
3. The erroneous belief that God sends suffering into our lives.
4. Our lack of understanding of what prayer is.

## A Subtle but Persistent "Who Has Sinned?" Mentality

We recall the story in the gospel of the man born blind. The question is asked, "Why is he blind?" Why should a human being suffer blindness? And, that question is followed by a second: "Who has sinned, this man or his parents?" (John 9:2)

I believe that some area of pain for the separated and divorced cannot be healed as long as the question that continues to be asked is: "Will God forgive me? I must have done something very sinful or my marriage would not have ended."

To view a broken marriage as a punishment for sin may be to short-circuit a growth to new life by never asking the important questions. Which is not to deny the role of human darkness and frailty, even of the human sinfulness that may be present in failure.

The point of the story of the blind man is that he had some special needs that had to be tended. Asking why he was blind was not particularly helpful. Jesus healed him.

Jesus was not concerned about why the man was blind.

Jesus says, "Neither he nor his parents have sinned." But the key to the story is in the words of Jesus that we may not háve noticed, or on which we may not have reflected. Jesus adds, "He was born blind so that the works of God might be revealed in him" (John 9:3). What Jesus is saying is that this suffering is an opportunity for the blind man to find the meaning of his life, to live his human life fully, and, in doing that, to find God's goodness and life.

## The Fallacy That God Loves Us Most When We Suffer

Somehow the message that has come to us as Christians is that God loves us when we suffer more than he loves us when we are happy. To the extent that we believe this, we are not faithful to the message of Jesus' own life, death and resurrection. Good Friday is not the central message of Jesus' life. Jesus walked through his death on Good Friday into an unknown future, but he walked through it to an Easter Sunday. The resurrection, Easter, our call to new life, to new hope, is the ultimate meaning of Jesus' life.

In our search for the meaning of suffering, we have risked being convinced of the less than human view that would have us believe that "If it hurts, it must be holy." From this follows the further belief that "The more it hurts, the holier I am or will be."

The truth is that God's invitation to each of us is to happiness and wholeness. Death and pain are realities, but the call is to life. The call is to journey with pain and darkness and death, when we must, but the journey leads to life. Jesus died but his words mean exactly what they say: "I have come so that they may have life and have it to the full" (John 10:10).

## The Erroneous Belief That God Sends Suffering into Our Lives

How often have we heard someone say, "God sent me this suffering because it is his will that I suffer"?

Suffering is not God-sent. Suffering is a reality of human life. It is a reality that arises out of our inability to see as far as we would like, our insecurity in facing the unknown, our fear as it flows over into the lives of others. Suffering enters our lives because of the accumulated cultural and social patterns in structures around us. The sources of suffering lie in ourselves and in others.

Suffering is not God-sent except insofar as God respects and will not interfere with his gift of human freedom. He allows us to use that gift for life or death, for joy or sadness, for happiness or for suffering through the decisions we make.

Suffering is not God-sent, but the love and strength that sustain and heal us are.

### Our Lack of Understanding of What Prayer Is

When pain and suffering become difficult companions for us, we often reach out to the place of love and strength that we know will always be there. We reach to find God. Our way of reaching for him is what we have called prayer. At times like these, we may distort and disfigure our own prayer unless ·we understand that prayer does not change God or others. If I promise prayers believing that, if I say enough prayers, God will do what I want him to do, that God will change another person, that God will make everything comfortable for me again, then I am not praying. There are many ways to pray, there are spoken and unspoken ways in which we look for and find God. None of these ways is a means to manipulate God so that he will interfere either with the human freedom of another person or change my life for me. Someone has said that "Prayer changes people and people, through prayer, find the strength and courage they need to change things, circumstances, and even themselves."

People who pray, expecting God to remove their pain or fix their broken lives, in the end, often hate God when he does not respond in the way they envision. People who pray, expecting to exercise some control over God, can only find frustration in such so-called prayer.

People who pray, struggling to find meaning and strength, reaching out to catch hold of their lives and to take responsibility for their decisions, come to love God. They come to love him because they find their own strength and goodness in his loving call to life.

Having thought about some of the barriers we place in our own way as we probe the mystery of suffering may help us to understand these obstacles or to identify others not mentioned here. Our purpose is not to dwell on the barriers but to see them for what they are. Our purpose is to look beyond them and to recognize the ways in which they have interfered with our finding meaning in Jesus' life and death, and in our own.

### We've Come to Learn the Secret and We'll Never Let It Go

These reflections on the mystery of suffering bring to mind a concert I attended given by the violinist, Isaac Stern. I was seated on the stage of Symphony Hall, facing Isaac Stern and his accompanist at a distance of not more than 15 feet. Because I was on the stage, I was in the unique position of being able to look out over the audience in that vast hall. As Isaac Stern began to play, I was quickly caught into a kind of aura that filled the hall. The faces of the thousands in that audience reflected far more than the fact that they were in the presence of a well-known violinist. The qualities of the man that touched all of us were more than the collective total of all the skills and knowledge, the personal discipline and time investment, the enthusiasm and commitment that are a part of the making of an artist.

I do not know the secret of Isaac Stern's life. I do not know the story of his human pilgrimage. I do know that he brought to us a personal presence that was much more than that of an artist who plays the violin superbly well. His manner, his facial expression, his attentiveness to his listeners, his whole body, all of who he is, somehow entered into and created the environment which surrounded us in that hall.

As I listened to him, I thought back to a violin concert I had attended about five years earlier. I remembered sitting in another hall with another large group of people. I also remembered the nearly sterile feeling in that hall. I left with the disappointment that neither my life nor that of others who were present seemed to have been touched in any significant way. The music lacked some combination of power and gentleness, of strength and fragility.

Since I do not know the details of what it is that makes great artists, except to know whether or not they have had an impact on me, I spoke to a professional musician who had been sitting not far from me during the concert. I said to her, "What happened tonight? What was it about that concert that left me feeling uninspired, untouched by some of my favorite compositions?" In her response she put into words what I could only feel in myself and in that crowd. She told me, "That man has probably one of the largest repertoires of difficult compositions committed to memory; his bowing and fingering skills are nearly flawless, but he remains a violin technician—not an artist."

Each of these men had known the study, the discipline, the long, exacting hours of practice, even the personal commitment to mastering the violin. One communicated richness and depth through the music he produced, giving the listener the feeling that this music was flowing out of some place very deep within him. The other was not capable of such communication with his audience and left them with the feeling that there is not a deep inner source out of which his music comes. One, by his presence, communicated meaning, the other did not.

Isaac Stern and the violin technician, the person who asks *how* and the one who asks only *why,* the searcher who cannot learn enough of giving and the frightened traveller who has already learned too much, the one who wants to explore the secret of Jesus' life and the one who flees, somehow sensing what it will ask—all of these make the same human journey. All of them walk in the ongoing exploration of the meaning of human life and, therefore, of its price. But each does it in a unique way and with a different sense of commitment and purpose. Each embraces giving and living with a different understanding of faithfulness to life.

Often we do not pursue the meaning of life or of death until we must, until some circumstance of life or of death demands that we do. Separated and divorced Catholics invested their lives in living and giving in a marriage they expected to last for as long as they lived. At some point they were forced to acknowledge the death of that same marriage, or at least its brokenness. They experienced both the dying and the living of Jesus. Theirs is no theoretical approach to the meaning of human suffering, for there is no easy way to deepen our understanding of life. There is no easy access to Jesus' secret.

What is the difference between Jesus and most other human beings who have lived? Each of us, like Jesus, experiences death and life as a part of the journey. Each of us knows the interplay of joy and sadness, of light and darkness, of security and fear, of love and rejection. We learn to recognize the tension places that bring us to the growing edges of our lives. Somehow all of these facets of human life, filtered through and flowing out of the life of Jesus challenge us to be open to all that Jesus can teach us about giving.

For Jesus, and for us if we choose that it shall be so, life comes together only when we allow our human experiences to enter deeply into our lives. We are most fully Christian when we are most truly human. And we are both Christian and human when we realize that if we will not walk in the companionship of suffering, then we cannot walk with love and happiness and joy for they are but different dimensions of the same life-giving companion.

*COME . . . DRY YOUR EYES NOW. . . .*